I0569636

Geshtunoör Occasional Papers Series

Geshtunoör Occasional Papers Series

No. 1 (2025)

The Dual High Priests of Luke 3:2

By

Alexander M. Frazier

Geshtunoör

Mauldin, SC

Copyright © 2025 by Geshtunoör Publishing

All rights reserved. No part of this publication may be reproduced, distributed, or transmitted in any form or by any means without the prior written permission of the publisher, except for brief quotations in critical reviews and certain other noncommercial uses permitted by copyright law.

Published by Geshtunoör Publishing
Mauldin, South Carolina
www.geshtunoor.com

Geshtunoör Occasional Papers Series, No. 1
ISSN: 3070-0949 (print)
ISSN: 3070-0957 (online)

ISBN: 978-1-971182-00-1 (paperback)
ISBN: 978-1-971182-01-8 (PDF)

Suggested citation: Frazier, Alexander M. "The Dual High Priests of Luke 3:2." *Geshtunoör Occasional Papers Series*, no. 1. Mauldin, SC: Geshtunoör Publishing, 2025.

Short form: Frazier, "The Dual High Priests of Luke 3:2," *GeshOPS* 1.

First edition, Dec. 2025

Printed in the United States of America

Library of Congress Control Number: 2025927674

Abstract

This work reopens the enigmatic case of the dual high priesthood of Luke 3:2, where Annas and Caiaphas are both subsumed under the singular title of high priest in contradiction to the legal exclusivity of high-priestly incumbency. This ostensibly incongruous statement by Luke has led to a variety of interpretive solutions over the centuries, ultimately culminating in the popular consensus view that Caiaphas held the official title while Annas was the true high priest behind the scenes. However, lacking any evidentiary foundation, this explanation proves to be an ad hoc rationalization that doesn't fare well under critical scrutiny. Viewed in its full historical context, Luke's statement actually reveals a remarkably precise and intimate understanding of the era's political landscape that is perfectly captured by his incisive articulation. By delving into the dynamics of Roman provincial administration and its impact on Jewish institutions, an obscure logistical reality emerges, providing a solution that is as historically robust as it is simple.

Abbreviations

Cic. *Att.*	Cicero, *Letters to Atticus*
CIL	*Corpus Inscriptionum Latinarum*
CJT	*Canadian Journal of Theology*
Dio Cass.	Dio Cassius, *Roman History*
Dion. Hal.	Dionysius of Halicarnassus, *Roman Antiquities*
Hieron. *Comm. Matt.*	Jerome, *Commentary on Matthew*
Joseph.	Josephus
AJ	*Antiquities of the Jews*
BJ	*Wars of the Jews*
Vit.	*Life*
JSJ	*Journal for the Study of Judaism*
Oros.	Orosius, *Seven Books of History Against the Pagans*
Ov. *Fast.*	Ovid, *Fasti*
P. Ryl.	*Rylands Papyri*
PL	*Patrologia Latina*
Philo *Leg.*	Philo, *Embassy to Gaius*
Suet. *Aug.*	Suetonius, *Life of Augustus*
Tac. *Ann.*	Tacitus, *Annals*

Bible Abbreviations

1 Macc.	1 Maccabees
Exod.	Exodus
Jn.	John
Lev.	Leviticus
Lk.	Luke
Mat.	Matthew
Mk.	Mark

Babylonian Talmud Abbreviations

bPesah.	Pesachim
bRosh Hash.	Rosh Hashana
bShabb.	Shabbat
bYoma	Yoma

Mishnah Abbreviations

mŠeqal.	Shekalim

Geshtunoör Occasional Papers Series

No. 1 (2025)

The Dual High Priests of Luke 3:2

By Alexander M. Frazier

The high priests of Luke 3:2 are an interesting case. The relevance of Luke's use of the high priests as a dating criterion delves into a poorly explored aspect of Jewish history, of which most casual readers are entirely ignorant. Luke situates the coming of John the Baptist during the high priesthood of Annas and Caiaphas, seemingly presenting them as a pair of joint officials holding the same office.[1] The problem with this, to get right to the point, is that it expresses an impossible scenario in Jewish legal culture. While Luke appears to suggest that there were two high priests at the same time, the fact is, there were never two concurrent high priests. Neither is there any evidence, explicit or implicit, to suggest otherwise by any dynamic or rationale.[2]

Given the universal recognition of this fact, the problem of Luke's statement, as you might expect, has become something of an enigma to New Testament scholarship. There is no denying what Luke is saying, but neither is there any documented primary-source exception to a singular office held by a single man. The closest we can get to this dynamic, apart from death—which does not apply to the men named in this circumstance—is mutilation, or ritual defilement, where one man was removed and another anointed in his stead, which would have resulted in two contemporaneous high priests.[3] However, these scenarios themselves exclude the possibility of two active high priests simultaneously. One is removed from the office

---

1. Lk. 3:2.

2. Fitzmyer, *Luke I–IX*, 458; Gill, *Exposition of the New Testament*, 1:483b–484a; McEachern, "Dual Witness and Sabbath Motif," *CJT* 12 (1966): 268.

3. Lev. 21:16–23; bYoma 12a–13a; Joseph. *AJ* 14.366, 17.165–166; Joseph. *BJ* 1.270.

before the other is appointed to it. And even these circumstances were rare.

The most common answer to the Luke conundrum, as Alfred Plummer so elegantly epitomized it, was that there was a high priest de jure and another de facto, meaning that while one held the official title, the other held the actual power behind the scenes.[1] This interpretation, which has become the predominant consensus on the matter, has been echoed by scholars such as Joseph Fitzmyer, F. F. Bruce, Craig Keener, Raymond Brown, and H. G. Enelow, and acknowledged, if not necessarily embraced, by scholars such as Vernon McEachern, John Gill et al.[2] It has become so popularly accepted that when asked why Luke names two high priests, modern artificial intelligence systems reflexively offer the de jure/de facto explanation as settled fact—often echoing it verbatim, showing just how extensively this point of view has taken root in popular academic culture. The perspective has even been subtly showcased in the television series, *The Chosen.*[3]

Nevertheless, despite its popularity, to the best of my knowledge, no one has provided a truly critical analysis to support the view, and, as noted, not all scholars agree with it. At its basest level, it is functionally no more than a commonsense deduction. When the hypothesis is subjected to critical scrutiny, there is not much to corroborate it. McEachern expressed the same sentiment, acknowledging that the interpretation was *possible*, but complaining that it had "too much of the ring of a modern rationalization to be completely convincing."[4] John Gill likewise criticized the interpretation's inconsistent assumption, questioning not only why Annas would be uniquely recognized as wielding the title and authority when other former high priests with equal claim were likely still living, but also why Luke would list him

---

1. Plummer, *Exegetical Commentary on Luke*, 84.

2. Fitzmyer, *Luke I–IX*, 458; Bruce, *Acts of the Apostles*, 150; Keener, *IVP Bible Background Commentary*, 299–300; Brown, *Gospel According to John: XIII–XXI*, 820–821; H. G. Enelow, "Annas," in *The Jewish Encyclopedia*, 1:610–611; McEachern, "Dual Witness and Sabbath Motif," *CJT* 12 (1966): 268; Gill, *Exposition of the New Testament*, 1:484a.

3. When queried about Luke's dual high priests, Google Gemini, Claude Sonnet, and ScholarGPT all offered the de jure/de facto explanation as settled fact. Although the articulation was slightly varied, the conclusions were the same across all formats.

4. McEachern, "Dual Witness and Sabbath Motif," *CJT* 12 (1966): 268.

as high priest in a year when he clearly was not serving in that capacity.[1]

In my own observation, which is similar to Gill's, I find that the interpretation is presumptuously negligent of the historical context, claiming that Annas retained de facto authority as "the true high priest in the eyes of the people," when the historical precedent points in a demonstrably different direction. If public sentiment genuinely favored any deposed high priest as a legitimate authority figure, it would have been Joazar, not Annas. Joazar was the last high priest approved and appointed by the people, and was, in fact, the first high priest since Alexander Jannaeus (105 BCE)—or arguably Aristobulus (69 BCE)—to have received the dignity of a legitimate appointment separate from the oversight of outside government authority.[2]

Joazar had been originally appointed by Herod after an incident where a seditious mob pulled down and destroyed a golden eagle

---

1. Gill, *Exposition of the New Testament*, 1:484a.

2. Beginning with Jonathan (Joseph. *AJ* 13.45–46; 1 Macc. 10:18–21), son of Mattathias (Joseph. *AJ* 12.265–266; 1 Macc. 2:1–5), the Hasmonean dynasty held the high priesthood in an unbroken chain—Jonathan to Simon (Joseph. *AJ* 13.196–201; 1 Macc. 13:23–42), Simon to John Hyrcanus I (Joseph. *AJ* 13.228–230; 1 Macc. 16:16–24), John Hyrcanus I to Aristobulus I (Joseph. *AJ* 13.301), Aristobulus I to Alexander Jannaeus (Joseph. *AJ* 13.320)—and had become a formally hereditary office beginning with Simon (Joseph. *AJ* 14.78; 1 Macc. 14:41–47). Alexander Jannaeus, the last to have legitimately inherited the titles of both king and high priest (Joseph. *AJ* 20.242), was survived and succeeded by his wife Alexandra (Joseph. *AJ* 13.400–407; Joseph. *BJ* 1.107), who appointed Hyrcanus high priest (Joseph. *AJ* 13.408, 20.242; Joseph. *BJ* 1.109), making Hyrcanus the first to be appointed by a monarch rather than naturally inheriting it. His brother Aristobulus then usurped both the throne and the high priesthood upon the death of Alexandra (Joseph. *AJ* 13.422–423, 14.4–7, 20.243; Joseph. *BJ* 1.117–119), making himself the final Hasmonean king and high priest to have taken both offices by right of blood, if not necessarily by right of succession, since Hyrcanus was the elder, as well as the intended heir (Joseph. *AJ* 13.408; Joseph. *BJ* 1.109, 120). Pompey then removed Aristobulus and reappointed Hyrcanus as the high priest (Joseph. *AJ* 14.73, 79; Joseph. *BJ* 1.153, 157). All other appointments following Hyrcanus, from Ananelus (Joseph. *AJ* 15.22), clear through to Matthias (Joseph. *AJ* 20.223), were the product of outside government interference, with the single exception of Joazar, who had the high priesthood conferred on him by the multitude (Joseph. *AJ* 18.26).

Herod had dedicated to the temple. Matthias was removed from the high priesthood, accused of complicity in the event, and was replaced by Joazar.[1] Archelaus later removed Joazar under suspicion of having aided in the uprising that had occurred while he was in Rome following Herod's death, and had appointed Eleazar in his place.[2] Jesus, son of Sie, then took Eleazar's place.[3] Years later, Archelaus was summoned to Rome, and we suddenly see Joazar back in the position of high priest upon the arrival of Quirinius, with no record of any succession.[4] The position, Josephus says, had been conferred on him "by the multitude"—not by Archelaus, who had removed him, nor by any Roman authority. The people themselves, in an act of insolent defiance to Archelaus' rule, had clearly deposed Jesus, son of Sie, and restored Joazar to the high priesthood on their own initiative, whose legitimacy they very obviously recognized and esteemed over Archelaus' chosen appointment.[5]

The fact is, the house of Boethus held dominance through an unbroken line, barring Jesus, son of Sie, whom the people readily removed. The line began with Simon, son of Boethus, followed by Matthias, brother-in-law to Joazar.[6] Matthias was replaced by Joazar, who was then replaced by Eleazar, his own brother, both of the house of Boethus.[7] Overall, the Boethus dynasty held power for thirty-one years, from approximately 24 BCE to 7 CE.[8]

Annas, by contrast, was the first Roman appointee installed—the Roman replacement for the people's choice—disparaging their brief exercise of independence scarcely before it got off the ground.[9] Given

---

1. Joseph. *AJ* 17.164.

2. Joseph. *AJ* 17.339.

3. Joseph. *AJ* 18.341.

4. Joseph. *AJ* 18.3.

5. Joseph. *AJ* 18.26. It is suggested that Joazar aided the seditious during Archelaus' absence following Herod's death (Joseph. *AJ* 17.339), showing Joazar to be a patriot. Joazar was also well enough esteemed that he was able to convince the Jews not to fight against the taxation being imposed by the Romans, though his influence was short-lived (Joseph. *AJ* 18.3–6).

6. Joseph. *AJ* 15.320–322, 17.78, 164.

7. Joseph. *AJ* 17.164, 167, 339.

8. Joseph. *AJ* 15.317; Dio Cass. 53.28.1, 53.29.3–8.

9. Joseph. *AJ* 18.26.

that the house of Annas is named after this patriarch, this was the foundation of their line, whereas the house of Boethus had existed for three decades. Since the concept we are dealing with here is the idea that the Roman appointment could not supersede the legitimate high priesthood in the eyes of the people, Joazar would have retained that status from the time Annas was appointed by Quirinius. So, the notion that Annas somehow retained the principal authority with the people after his own deposition rather than Joazar, who had been restored by popular will, is especially illogical. If anyone embodied legitimate authority behind the scenes, grounded in popular sentiment and perceptions of legitimacy, it would have been the man the people collectively chose as their high priest, not the Roman appointee who displaced him.

Additionally, to further quash this notion, Gill, as I briefly noted, argued that besides Annas, a lingering claim to high-priesthood status could have been equally made not only for Joazar, but also for Ishmael, Eleazar, and Simeon, who were all relatively recent former high priests.[1] Annas was hardly a unique figure at this juncture. It cannot even be argued that wealth and prestige were the basis for Annas' political dominance. The house of Boethus, to which Joazar belonged, was equally prominent and wealthy, and probably more so after thirty years of direct connection with the royal family.[2] They already had a firm foothold and continued to exert authoritative sway well into the mid-first century.[3] Again, if ongoing public sentiment for a deposed high priest had a genuine influence on the perception of high-priestly legitimacy in the eyes of the public, absent the official title, Joazar—not Annas—would have been the natural candidate for such popular affection.

But all of this assumes that such behind-the-scenes authority existed in the first place. The Bible makes no such claim, stated or implied. Neither do any of the extrabiblical sources. The closest we can come to "evidence" in this matter is Josephus, in whose work we find

---

1. Gill, *Exposition of the New Testament*, 1:484a.

2. Joseph. *AJ* 15.317, 320–322; Dio Cass. 53.28.1, 53.29.3–8. Simon, son of Boethus, was elevated to high priest by Herod in 24 BCE to make the family of suitable aristocratic stature for Herod to marry Simon's daughter.

3. Joseph. *AJ* 18.26, 19.297; Joseph. *BJ* 5.527; bPesah. 57a.

instances of former high priests being referred to as "high priest," supporting at the very least the emeritus concept, which is the circumstantial principle from which Annas' alleged authority is derived.[1] Josephus, in many cases, mentions multiple high priests in the plural, showing the retained epithet for more than one person, and frequently in contexts where there is a known and appointed high priest for the contemporary period in question.[2]

However, despite any superficial appearances to the contrary, Josephus is not narrating a system that violates fundamental Jewish law and custom. There could be only one high priest at a time, and a careful exegesis of Josephus' examples clearly reveals an authority structure that subordinates even these apparent emeritus high priests under a singular individual.

One particularly illuminating example appears in Josephus' account concerning Jesus, son of Damneus, Ananias, and some other "high priests" during the procuratorship of Albinus. The context gives us a working example of titles, authority, and subordination.

> Agrippa took the high priesthood from him [Ananus, son of Ananus], when he had ruled but three months, and made Jesus, the son of Damneus, high priest. Now, as soon as Albinus was come to the city of Jerusalem, he used all his endeavors and care that the country might be kept in peace, and this by destroying many of the *sicarii*; but as for the high priest Ananias, he increased in glory every day, and this to a great degree, and had obtained the favor and esteem of the citizens in a signal manner; for he was a great hoarder up of money; he therefore cultivated the friendship of Albinus, and of the high priest [Jesus], by making them presents; he also had servants who were very wicked, who joined themselves to the boldest sort of the people, and went to the thrashing floors, and took away the tithes that belonged to the priests by violence, and did not refrain from beating such as would not give these tithes to them. So the other high priests acted in the like manner, as did those

---

1. Bruce, *Acts of the Apostles*, 150. Bruce appears to argue synonymy between seniority and the honor of emeritus status, stating, "Even after his deposition Annas enjoyed great prestige; by this time he was senior ex-high priest (or, as we might say, high priest emeritus)." Although not directly stated, Bruce implies that Annas was unique in this regard, though the evidence does prove differently.

2. Joseph. *AJ* 20.205, 207–208; Joseph. *Vit*. 193–194; Joseph. *BJ* 4.151, 6.114.

his servants without anyone being able to prohibit them; so that [some of the] priests, that of old were wont to be supported with those tithes, died for want of food.[1]

We have a clear delineation of a singular high priest, Jesus, son of Damneus, whom Ananias, the "high priest"—a former high priest five successions prior—sought to curry favor with by means of presents. The behavior of Ananias' servants, robbing the priests of the tithes, was then mimicked by the other "high priests."[2] Although we have a single, definitive high priest appointed by Agrippa, we nevertheless have numerous individuals recognized as high priests, though they are subordinate to *the* high priest, as demonstrated by Ananias, who presumably cultivated a type of informal *clientela* with both Jesus and Albinus, two recognized figures of authority who outranked him.

The New Testament itself just as readily showcases this same sort of titular ambiguity that we find in Josephus, though the average reader would be entirely unaware of it. It repeatedly refers to the ἀρχιερεῖς, or "high priests," in the plural, while maintaining a definitive, singular high priest who is clearly separate from the plurality.

In answer to this, the New Testament translators offer us an elegant solution to the problem, albeit at the potential expense of inadvertently obscuring a subtlety of the priestly culture. Whereas the text of Josephus is translated literally, causing the undeniable confusion we are currently addressing, the New Testament translators have resorted to a more interpretive rendering, calling them "chief priests" in these instances to disambiguate them from the high priest himself. The fact is, both sources are working with the word ἀρχιερεῖς, which is "high priests" in the plural, suggesting either multiple simultaneous officeholders—*extremely* unlikely—or multiple men who were not *the* high priest, though they nevertheless had or retained the title of "high priest" regardless.

This very concept, albeit in a far more limited application, is the beating heart of the emeritus hypothesis concerning Annas and his retained authority. Unfortunately, the reality of the far more

---

1. Joseph. *AJ* 20.203–207.

2. Joseph. *AJ* 20.103, 203–207.

widespread scope of the title being shared by numerous individuals naturally engenders an inherent and unavoidable irony in the sense that multiplying the number of individuals bearing a similar emeritus title dilutes the claim to any unique authority. If every former high priest retained the title, but none held the office, what gives one high priest more authority than another high priest, when neither is *the* high priest? As the saying goes, if everyone is special, no one is.

The logical implication of this should also be considered. If Annas is being referred to as the high priest alongside Caiaphas on the basis of his emeritus status, as is so often suggested, that particular criterion inherently demands an explanation for the exclusion of all the other emeritus high priests. While the question risks an *argumentum ex silentio*, the rhetoric itself exposes the self-evident absurdity of this point of view. Why would Luke not write, "in the high priesthood of Joazar, Annas, Ismael, Eleazar, Simon, and Caiaphas," since the ἀρχιερεῖς usage applied to all of them? Unless Annas was somehow preeminent among the former high priests—which we have already established was not the case—the simple explanation of an emeritus title offers no principled impetus for Luke's exclusive pairing of Annas with Caiaphas. It is, in fact, entirely arbitrary.

But that aside, granting the recognition of these "high priests," in Josephus and in the Bible, there is nevertheless a clearly delineated authority structure. Case in point, we have instances such as that of Mark, where the high priest, the high priests, and the elders are all represented together, demonstrating distinct social classes and a hierarchy.

> And they led Jesus away to the high priest (τὸν ἀρχιερέα): and with him were assembled all the chief priests (οἱ ἀρχιερεῖς) and the elders (οἱ πρεσβύτεροι) and the scribes.[1]

It was all very stratified. At the apex stood ὁ ἀρχιερεύς—the high priest, the singular incumbent of the highest office. Beneath him were οἱ ἀρχιερεῖς—literally "the high priests," testified by Josephus as the aristocratic succession families from which the high priest himself was selected, all of whom, according to the blatant title, had or

---

1. Mk. 14:53.

retained high-priestly status, if not necessarily the office or authority.[1] These were not merely senior priests, as the term "chief priests" would imply. These were the aristocracy, the highest tier of the priestly caste. They were the high priest's peers and equals, and were subordinate to him only relative to incumbency. Below them came οἱ πρεσβύτεροι—the presbyters, the council of elder priests, not to be confused with the chief priests who held their rank by virtue of hereditary right rather than age. And so we have the high priest, the high priests, and the elders.

This same grouping is again attested to in Matthew, representing the high priest, the high priests, along with the elders and the scribes.

> Then assembled together the chief priests (οἱ ἀρχιερεῖς), and the scribes, and the elders (οἱ πρεσβύτεροι) of the people, unto the palace of the high priest (τοῦ ἀρχιερέως), who was called Caiaphas.[2]

All in all, the chief priests, properly the "high priests" in the plural, are mentioned at least sixty-five times throughout the New Testament.[3] As such, all notions of authority as the high priest in principle behind the scenes due to an emeritus title ought to be permanently retired. They *all* maintained the title as part of their aristocratic class. It was by no means a novel phenomenon, and therefore has no bearing on any perceived authority Annas may have allegedly retained. In all cases, the context and comparisons clearly indicate a broader caste of high priests operating collectively in political and religious affairs, separate from the high priest's office itself, but recognized nonetheless as "high priests."

An additional example of this distinction can be seen in the instance of Ananus during the high priesthood of Ananias. Both are called high priests, but only Ananias was *the* high priest, while

---

1. Joseph. *BJ* 4.147.

2. Mat. 26:3.

3. Mat. 2:4, 16:21, 20:18, 21:15, 21:23, 21:45, 26:3, 26:14, 26:47, 26:59, 27:1, 27:3, 27:6, 27:12, 27:20, 27:41, 27:62, 28:11; Mk. 8:31, 10:33, 11:18, 11:27, 14:1, 14:10, 14:43, 14:53, 14:55, 15:1, 15:3, 15:10, 15:11, 15:31; Lk. 9:22, 19:47, 20:1, 20:19, 22:2, 22:4, 22:52, 22:66, 23:4, 23:10, 23:13, 23:23, 24:20; Jn. 7:32, 7:45, 11:47, 11:57, 12:10, 18:3, 18:35, 19:6, 19:15, 19:21; Acts 4:23, 5:24, 9:14, 9:21, 22:30, 23:14, 25:2, 25:15, 26:10, 26:12.

Ananus' official role, even as a "high priest," was commander/governor (στρατηγέω) of the temple, not far removed from the similar suggestions of authority made by Edersheim, Gill, Ellicott et al.[1] Although Ananus, from an *emeritus* standpoint, would have permanently retained the title of high priest after his deposition, his exercisable authority would have been subject to the limitations of whatever office he might have held. The high-priestly authority was vested in a single man, Ananias in this instance, with Ananus' authority being the governor of the temple, *not* that of the high seat, whatever honorary title he may have held, incidentally demonstrating that he did not maintain the true high priesthood behind the scenes, but was demonstrably subordinate to the government-appointed high priest.[2]

The contextual distinction between the plural collective and the singular office is explicit. Again, Bible translators have long recognized this, which is why they chose to translate ἀρχιερεῖς in the

---

1. Joseph. *AJ* 20.131, 208; Edersheim, *Life and Times of Jesus*, 565–566; Gill, *Exposition of the New Testament*, 1:484a–484b; Ellicott, *New Testament Commentary*, 260; Henry, *Commentary*, 611; Clarke, *New Testament*, on Luke 3:2; Jamieson, Fausset, and Brown, *Commentary on the Old and New Testaments*, 2:101–102.

2. The identification of this Ananus serving as the commander of the temple is nuanced, but can be determined as Ananus, son of Seth, by the onomastic connection to Eleazar (Joseph. *AJ* 20.131, 20.208, 18.34). Although some would argue that the Eleazar in this instance is Eleazar, son of Ananus, son of Ananias—a lineage nowhere else directly mentioned—the perceived synonymy of Ananus, commander of the temple (Joseph. *AJ* 20.131) and Ananus, son of Ananias (Joseph. *BJ* 2.243), is assumptive to the homonymy rather than absolute, and can be further attributed to the presumption that Ananus, son of Seth, died circa 40 CE, which is nowhere attested to—he is, in fact, mentioned in the immediately preceding context. The alleged patronymic relationship between Ananus, Eleazar, and Ananias is never elucidated by Josephus in this context, and is contradicted by the *sicarii* promising to return "the scribe" (Joseph. *AJ* 20.209) rather than Ananias' kin, by whatever familial term one may choose to use. Their continued endeavors to kidnap other "servants" (Joseph. *AJ* 20.210) likewise relegates Eleazar to the status of a temple official generally, showing that they were not necessarily targeting family members, but those serving in the temple under Ananias, who appears to have been "Rabbi Ḥananya, the deputy High Priest," or *sagan* (mŠeqal. 6:1), whom we are informed cultivated a relationship with Albinus, explaining on two fronts, not only why they would extort him specifically, but why they would abduct temple officials to do it.

Biblical passages as "chief priests" in these plural constructions, to preserve the institutional separation.

So, when we consider the "evidence" of Josephus or the Bible supporting the emeritus concept through examples of former high priests retaining the title, or exercising concurrent authority in the plural, it does not prove what some might suggest it proves. What the evidence demonstrates is an aristocracy of prominent succession families, out of which the high priest's office was filled.[1]

Modern scholarship has increasingly recognized this institutional reality. M. Stern, surveying the evidence of who could be designated ἀρχιερεῖς, concluded that, "at the close of the Second Temple period, any distinguished priest, distinguished by reason of his social standing, and in a majority of instances, one who belonged to the group of oligarchical priestly families of the high priesthood could be called a high priest." He further notes that, "what was decisive was not the specific function in the administration of the Temple but one's general social standing," observing that, "the term high priests serves as an expression *par excellence* of the social hierarchy that prevailed at the end of the Second Temple period," and, "reflects the collective superiority of the oligarchical class of the priesthood."[2]

Stern's analysis, in other words, confirms what Josephus explicitly states, that the ἀρχιερεῖς constituted a defined institutional class—the "oligarchical priestly families"—who held recognized succession rights to the highest office. While Stern frames this somewhat broadly as "distinguished priests" of high social standing, titles *par excellence*, the point nevertheless remains that they were recognized as the highest social class. They held the high-priestly title because of who they were, and they differed from the high priest himself, again, solely in the sense of incumbency to the high seat.

In short, what presents as the true practice of the time is that both former and future high priests *all* had, and retained, the high-priestly titles and status. This was a matter of family heritage. There are simply too many examples to ignore this reality. However, absent the authority of the supreme office itself, they were merely part of the collective caste, deriving their authority from lesser offices, such as

---

1. Joseph. *BJ* 4.148.

2. Stern, "Aspects of Jewish Society," in *Jewish People in the First Century*, 2:603.

the governor of the temple.[1] Only one was the ἀρχιερεὺς of the ἀρχιερέων—the high priest of the high priests—at any given time. And from this perspective, considering the complicated dynamics, perhaps the Bible translators were wise to disambiguate the term by calling them "chief priests" rather than the literal "high priests," though, again, I think important subtleties of the true priestly culture have been obscured in so doing.

Ultimately, the evidence for any recognition of former high priests retaining the high-priestly authority in the sense that some claim Luke 3:2 implies is sorely lacking and frequently contradicted. There are plenty of examples of men being called high priests, including, and especially, former officeholders. However, these were nevertheless demonstrably subordinate to the highest office and did not themselves wield that authority.

Stepping back from this, what does need to be recognized is that Luke 3:2 differs from the examples we have addressed, given that his statement suggests via the singular phraseology that the two men were both *the* high priest, the ἀρχιερεὺς of the ἀρχιερέων—dual incumbents to the singular high seat. As Plummer states:

> "Under the high priest Annas-Caiaphas," which means that between them they discharged the duties, or that each of them in different senses was regarded high priest [...][2]

This example in Luke is the only instance in all of the literature, Biblical or otherwise, where two or more men are implied both contextually and linguistically to have held the specific office of the high priest, in its full application and authority, simultaneously.

The passage is both unique and anomalous, and is the sole catalyst for the entire de jure/de facto point of view. Without it, the hypothesis would not even exist. The grammatical singularity and the conclusion it implies are precisely why scholars have found the passage enigmatic. Luke's phrasing suggests that two individuals somehow shared the unique office of the high priest during the timeframe he describes. It was the high priesthood of Annas and Caiaphas.

---

1. Joseph. *AJ* 20.131.

2. Plummer, *Exegetical Commentary on Luke*, 84.

All other Biblical references to these two men, whether individually or together, designate only one as high priest at any given time, while the other is merely identified by familial relation, or not mentioned at all.[1] Luke 3:2 is truly and wholly isolated in this, and the unavoidable confusion it creates has prompted authors like McEachern, Wolter, and Mason to suggest that, perhaps, Luke simply did not know who the high priest really was.[2]

Ultimately, there is not a shred of Christian, Jewish, or secular evidence to support two high priests at the same time, in any sense of the word, apart from the dynamics of the aristocracy as already discussed. The closest we might come to enforceable political authority absent the high seat is the almost mafia-like dynastic power and influence the house of Annas wielded, but, again, this sort of authority was exercised by several priestly families to their mutual discredit, including the house of Boethus, a rival to the house of Annas, with better popular support from the people.[3] The scholarly consensus in all its variations rests entirely on Luke 3:2, absent a stitch of historical corroboration, essentially amounting to little more than fiat.

The Contextual Arguments

In the interest of objectivity, I do have to say that there are *contextual* arguments that have been made to support the dual high priesthood. However, these arguments should be rightly evaluated according to the principles already established. First, there could only be one high priest at any given time. Any argument suggesting otherwise is suspect. Secondly, the emeritus title did not grant any actual high-priestly authority. Nor was it unique. It was shared by many individuals, and there is no precedent for Luke to single out Annas among the rest, negating this understanding as the logic behind Luke's statement. Thirdly, any authority a former high priest held was relative to whatever position he occupied, as in the case of Ananus serving as the governor of the temple during the high priesthood of Ananias.

---

1. Mat. 26:3, 26:57; Jn. 11:49, 18:13, 18:24; Acts 4:6.

2. McEachern, "Dual Witness and Sabbath Motif," *CJT* 12 (1966): 268; Wolter, *The Gospel According to Luke*, 1:159; Mason, *Josephus and the New Testament*, 130.

3. Joseph. *AJ* 18.26; bPesah. 57a.

Lastly, if Annas' supposed authority was a perceptual issue in the eyes of the public, that preeminence more properly belongs to Joazar. His was the last high priesthood properly attained, whereas Annas' high priesthood was the first of the illegitimate ones sanctioned by Rome, making Joazar's high priesthood the *only* one to qualify for the concept of public perception as described by that particular argument.

Nevertheless, three significant contextual arguments are often made in an attempt to demonstrate that both men were equally recognized as the high priest in the sense of mutual authority, as presented by Luke, and they deserve to be heard and answered.

The Interrogation

In the first place, a casual reader might object that John 18:13–24 appears to identify Annas as high priest, corroborating the "principle" concept of his retained authority behind the scenes. The argument in a nutshell is that Jesus is interrogated by the high priest, but he is at the house of Annas. Annas is therefore the high priest, as is Caiaphas.[1] Fitzmyer and Mason both embrace this argument, based precisely on this set of Scripture, claiming Annas had the title of high priest relative primarily to John 18:13 and 18:19.[2] However, this interpretation is poorly conceived and an unfortunate byproduct of the anachronistic statement in John 18:24, that "Annas had sent him bound unto Caiaphas the high priest," which gives the impression that the interrogation took place before Jesus was sent to Caiaphas, as Mason argues specifically.[3] The exegesis is neglectful of the overall context. John 18:24—that he had been bound and sent to Caiaphas—is a retrospective statement to establish the temporal context of the interrogation and trial. The past-perfect tense, "had sent," explicitly qualifies the events just narrated as having occurred under the conditions of the qualifier. In other words, the reason Jesus is shown being interrogated by the high priest isn't that Annas was the high priest, but that Annas had sent him bound *to* the high priest, Caiaphas.

In actual fact, the narrative sequence itself, if you follow it carefully, unambiguously reveals that the interrogation recorded in John

---

1. Jn. 18:13, 19, 22.

2. Fitzmyer, *Luke I–IX*, 458; cf. Edersheim, *Life and Times of Jesus*, 183.

3. Mason, *Josephus and the New Testament*, 130.

18:19–23 was conducted by Caiaphas, not Annas, despite the opinions of scholars like Fitzmyer and Mason who contend otherwise.[1] The contextual specifics, to borrow a phrase from Whiston, are beyond rational contradiction. In John 18:15, *after* Jesus had been led away first to Annas (18:13), Peter then followed Jesus into "the palace of the high priest"—a description that matches Matthew 26:58, Mark 14:54, and Luke 22:54, all of which place Peter at the high priest's residence, identified by Matthew as that of Caiaphas.[2] The interrogation and trial recorded in John 18:19–23 correspond directly to those described in Matthew 26:59–68, Mark 14:55–65, and Luke 22:63–65. All four Gospels describe the same sequence of events, including Peter's denials, and they all occur at the same location. Because of their conspicuous textual synonymy, John is clearly telling the same story, and 18:24 is just a poorly understood addendum. The four Gospels become instantly harmonious when it is acknowledged that these events all took place at the palace of the high priest Caiaphas, where Annas had sent Jesus bound for trial.

Taken to Annas First

The second contextual lure is a bit stronger. One might ask why Jesus was taken to Annas rather than Caiaphas. Arguably, it could be inferred that Annas had some authority of significance, just as mainstream scholarship suggests. In other words, they did not go directly to Caiaphas because Annas was the *true* authority behind the scenes.

But the answer to this is far simpler, and much more boring, than the intricate theories of secret government authorities operating from the shadows. The reason Jesus was initially taken to Annas really just comes down to the chain of command. The whole scenario revolves around laws, protocols, rank, and priestly hierarchy. Judas did not make his deal with the high priest himself, but with the chief priests (literally, "high priests," with the Biblical language retained here for disambiguation). It wasn't the high priest who sent the Jewish officers to arrest Jesus. They were dispatched by the chief priests. When Judas repented, he did not return the silver to the high priest. He returned it

---

1. Fitzmyer, *Luke I–IX*, 458; Mason, *Josephus and the New Testament*, 130.
2. Mat. 26:57–58.

to the chief priests.[1] Generals don't command and discipline privates. They send their instructions down through the chain of command. Jesus' arrest was properly orchestrated and executed by the chief priests in every respect, of whom Annas undoubtedly served in some senior capacity, possibly even as the governor of the temple, as we see later during the high priesthood of Ananias.

Annas came from one of the most powerful priestly families of the era and had himself served as high priest before being deposed. After his removal, both his son Eleazar and his son-in-law Caiaphas held the office within four years, and eventually most of the sons of Annas would serve as high priest, establishing what was essentially a priestly dynasty.[2] As the head of such a high-priestly family, coupled with years of experience, the wisdom of age, and a son-in-law currently serving as high priest at the time in question, I have every confidence that Annas would have served at the top of the hierarchy among the chief priests.

Gill, and others of his contemporary era—Charles Ellicott, Matthew Henry, Adam Clarke, Robert Jamieson et al—suggest that he may have held the formal position of *sagan*—a deputy priest who stood at the high priest's right hand, with all the other priests under his authority, save the high priest himself.[3] Josephus, as I previously pointed out, later explicitly identifies Annas as holding the title "commander of the temple" during the high priesthood of Ananias. Although not necessarily the *sagan*, this title falls within the scope of Gill's argument of alternate high-level authority, and would have been precisely the sort of title and authority necessary to have initiated an arrest.[4] Edersheim, too, argues a similar case, that "the conjunction of the two names of Annas and Caiaphas probably indicates that, although Annas was deprived of the Pontificate, he still continued to preside over the Sanhedrin," allowing, according to Acts 4:6, that Annas was the "president" of the Sanhedrin, identified earlier in his work as being synonymous with the *nasi*. The same official identification

---

1. Mat. 26:14–15, 26:47, 27:3–8; Mk. 14:10–11, 14:43; Lk. 22:4–6, 22:52–53.

2. Joseph. *AJ* 18.26, 18.34–35, 20.198.

3. Gill, *Exposition of the New Testament*, 1:484a–484b; Ellicott, *New Testament Commentary*, 260; Henry, *Commentary*, 611; Clarke, *New Testament*, on Luke 3:2; Jamieson, Fausset, and Brown, *Commentary on the Old and New Testaments*, 2:101–102.

4. Joseph. *AJ* 20.131.

is likewise offered as a potential, albeit erroneous, solution by both Ellicott and Henry.[1]

Although none of these authors—Gill, Ellicott, Henry, Clarke, Edersheim et al—credibly address Luke's precise terminology of ἀρχιερεύς—high priest—which is functionally and linguistically distinct from *sagan, nasi* (president of the Sanhedrin), or even *av beit din* (vice-president of the Sanhedrin), their suggestions concerning his position of authority within the priestly hierarchy do helpfully illuminate the precedent—in the *absence* of the high priesthood—for Jesus being brought to him first. It is a straightforward chain-of-command issue, not evidence of retained high-priestly authority. This is especially apparent with the "high priest" title very blatantly omitted from Annas and applied to Caiaphas instead.

Whether Annas actually held a formal title as the commentators suggest—and which is quite probable according to Josephus' later testimony—or whether he simply wielded the corresponding authority of one by virtue of his pedigree and experience, he was nevertheless a man of significant standing. He would have been the natural coordinator of Jesus' apprehension. If temple soldiers were sent to carry out the arrest, he would have been the one who sent them.

So, while some interpreters view the decision to bring Jesus first to Annas as implicit evidence of his retained authority as "high priest in principle," it is really nothing more than the officers observing an established chain of command. Annas was the ranking chief priest. In truth, what would have actually been historically awkward would have been for the temple soldiers to bypass the lower ranks and deliver Jesus to the high priest directly.

Annas the High Priest

---

1. Edersheim, *Life and Times of Jesus*, 67, 182–183; Ellicott, *New Testament Commentary*, 260; Henry, *Commentary*, 611. The *nasi* perspective contradicts the evidence. The Hillel dynasty held the *Nesiut* by hereditary right for a hundred years prior to the destruction of Jerusalem. It was held by Hillel, Simon ben Hillel, Gamaliel ben Simon, and Simon ben Gamaliel (bPesach. 66a; bShabb. 15a; Segal, "Intercalation and the Hebrew Calendar," *VT* 7.3 (July 1957): 259–260). The actual *nasi* contemporary to Annas in the Luke 3:2 context was Simon ben Hillel.

The third, and by far the soundest, piece of contextual evidence for the dual high priesthood is Annas actually being called the high priest in Acts 4:5–6 in a context that blatantly suggests he was *the* high priest, and not merely an honorary high priest emeritus.

> And it came to pass on the morrow, that their rulers, and elders, and scribes, and Annas the high priest, and Caiaphas, and John, and Alexander, and as many as were of the kindred of the high priest, were gathered together at Jerusalem.

Practically speaking, this illustrates the very problem we are dealing with, which is what makes this such a compelling piece of contextual evidence. Via Josephus, we know that Caiaphas was appointed by Valerius Gratus in 20 CE and deposed by Lucius Vitellius in 37 CE.[1] If Caiaphas was the known and official high priest throughout that duration, and Annas was nevertheless being outright called the high priest prior to Caiaphas' dismissal, then this would be proof of both men holding the office.

What's more, it is not even being presented from an emeritus point of view. Annas is being directly titled. The grammatical expression of the hierarchy here could not be much more explicit or deliberate. In Acts 4:5–6, we have the rulers, the elders, the scribes, Annas

---

1. Joseph. *AJ* 18.35, 18.95. While it is cited by rote that Gratus came into Judaea in 15 CE, and that Caiaphas was first appointed in 18 CE, the overlapping administrations of Pilate and Gratus demonstrate that Gratus came in 17 CE. At no point is it directly stated when Gratus came into Judaea. Josephus merely says that, "He [Tiberius] was now the third emperor; and he sent Valerius Gratus to be procurator of Judea, and to succeed Annius Rufus" (Joseph. *AJ* 18.33). But he does not say when, except that it was at the conclusion of Rufus' term, whenever that was. It is merely assumed that Tiberius sent him immediately. However, Pilate served ten inclusive years, ending shortly before Nisan of 37 CE, since he left for Rome not long before the death of Tiberius (Joseph. *AJ* 18.89). That makes the first year of his tenure the year beginning in Nisan of 27 CE, with his final year beginning in Nisan of 36 CE. Pilate's first year overlaps Gratus' eleventh year (Joseph. *AJ* 18.35), making the first year of Gratus' tenure the year beginning in Nisan of 17 CE, with his final year beginning in Nisan of 27, when Pilate came to succeed him. Caiaphas was appointed in Gratus' fourth year (Joseph. *AJ* 18.35), making Caiaphas the high priest from the year beginning in Nisan of 20 CE. Hypotheses to the contrary notwithstanding, this is the documented fact of the matter.

the high priest, and those of "high-priestly lineage"—i.e. οἱ ἀρχιερεῖς—the high priests. This is virtually identical to what we see in Mark 14:53 and Matthew 26:3. Annas was not merely one of those "of high-priestly descent"—one of the high-priestly caste—else he would have been included without distinction—"... and Annas, and Caiaphas, and John . . . and as many others that were of high-priestly lineage." Instead, Luke distinguishes him with the definitive title.[1]

This brings us back full circle to the original problem. Two men could not occupy the position of high priest at the same time, which I would argue is borne out and corroborated in this instance by the fact that Caiaphas is absent the title. I do not believe this was an accident or an oversight. Annas was the high priest, while Caiaphas and the others, separately, are tied expressly to the high-priestly aristocracy we have already discussed at length, via the circumlocution "those of high-priestly descent," the identity of which is definitively clarified by Josephus.[2] Although English translations commonly render this, "of the kindred of the high priest," making it appear that Luke is describing Annas and his immediate, and possibly extended, family, this is incorrect. The Greek identifies a class, or *genus*—those of high-priestly lineage—not a specific familial relationship to Annas himself. Such a rendering would require a grammatical structure not present in this passage.[3] Caiaphas and the others—though historically his relatives in truth—are tied not to Annas in this instance, but to those that Scripture elsewhere calls the "chief priests," demonstrating Caiaphas' categorical subordination rather than his equality.

Furthermore, if Annas being named high priest in the instance of Acts 4:6 was evidence of dual high-priestly authority, the mutual

---

1. Mason, *Josephus and the New Testament*, 129–130. Mason makes almost the same argument, that Luke includes Caiaphas among the high-priestly family, while Annas is implied to be the serving high priest.

2. Joseph. *BJ* 4.148.

3. In ἐκ γένους ἀρχιερατικοῦ, γένους is the noun, while ἀρχιερατικοῦ is a modifying adjective. For the phrase to correctly say, "of the kindred of the high priest," it would rightly be ἐκ τοῦ γένους τοῦ ἀρχιερέως, representing τοῦ γένους (of the lineage, *n.*, *gen. sing.*) with the definite article, and τοῦ ἀρχιερέως (of the high priest, *n.*, *gen. sing.*), also with the definite article. That is not what we have here. There is no grammatical tie between those, "of high-priestly (ἀρχιερατικοῦ, adj.) lineage (γένους, n.)" and Annas.

presence of Annas and Caiaphas both in the Acts scene was the perfect opportunity for Luke to reiterate the shared office and power allegedly expressed in Luke 3:2, since Luke authored both works. He could easily have said, "Annas and Caiaphas, the high priests, and John, and Alexander ..." Instead, he drops Caiaphas' title and groups him with the high priests generally, being among ὅσοι ἦσαν ἐκ γένους ἀρχιερατικοῦ, "all those of high-priestly lineage," applying the high-priestly title itself to Annas exclusively.

Ultimately, rather than Acts 4:6 being proof that Annas and Caiaphas were both the high priest at the same time, by whatever ad hoc mechanism might be imagined, I would contend that the Greek of this passage presents a clear juxtaposition between Annas having the title versus Caiaphas being reduced to holding a title no greater than his association with the high-priestly lineages, demonstrating that the high priesthood had changed hands, despite the appearance of Caiaphas' continuous tenure through to his eventual dismissal.

The fact is, had Luke named any other high priest, such as Ananias or Theophilus, we would not even be having this discussion. It would be taken as read that the high priesthood had changed hands, which would present a different set of speculations. The commentaries would be full of hypotheses on how it was that Ananias, or Theophilus, or whomever, was the high priest in the midst of Caiaphas' administration, and they would be conjuring up all manner of explanations to show how and why Caiaphas had been displaced for a period of time to accommodate this other plainly stated high priest.

But because we are dealing with Annas, there is an automatic presumption relative to Luke 3:2 that this is proof of both men serving as high priest—except that two men could not serve as high priest at the same time, barring the misguided and imaginative version where Annas had some illogical, unattested, and undocumented principal authority that he retains nowhere else.

In this case, Annas alone held the title of high priest in Acts 4:6, whereas Caiaphas very plainly lacked the title himself. While it would appear from Josephus that Caiaphas had an uninterrupted administration through 37 CE, this was obviously not the case—though his later dismissal by Vitellius demonstrates that he clearly regained the high priesthood prior to 37 CE.

Nevertheless, at this specific point in the narrative, the high priesthood had changed hands, and this is the key to the puzzle.

Understanding the Dual High Priesthood

Where most interpretations of Luke 3:2 fail is in assuming concurrency, which is an easy mistake to fall prey to, given the presentation. However, Luke was not insisting that they were both the high priest at the same time. He was informing us that they were both the high priest in the same year. That is the actual context, and is therefore the context in which it should be evaluated. John the Baptist came in the fifteenth year of the reign of Tiberius Caesar, and all the chronological anchors attached to that statement need to be viewed within the bounds of that parameter. Pontius Pilate was governor of Judaea in the fifteenth year of Tiberius. Herod was tetrarch of Galilee, Philip the tetrarch of Ituraea and the region of Trachonitis, and Lysanias the tetrarch of Abilene in the fifteenth year of Tiberius. And Annas and Caiaphas were both the high priest in the fifteenth year of Tiberius. In other words, he was saying that there were two high priests, first Annas, and then Caiaphas, in the year John the Baptist came out publicly—a circumstance repeated in Acts 4:6, just in reverse. The year of Acts 4:6 could be rightly called the year of the high priesthood of Caiaphas and Annas. Caiaphas was the high priest through the date of the crucifixion, and Annas was the high priest beginning sometime after Pentecost. This dynamic answers directly to Mason's inquiry concerning the order in which Annas and Caiaphas are listed in Luke 3:2.

> If we suppose that Annas, as a former high priest of distinction, offered the serving high priest his ongoing counsel, we are still left with the problem that Caiaphas' name should have appeared first; having been in office for a decade or more, he was no novice. In this awkward construction, however, the name of Caiaphas is left dangling, and it seems that Luke thinks of Annas as the high priest.[1]

This awkward and problematic construction Mason detects is the result of a subjective perception of order according to rank and priority. In actual fact, Annas is mentioned first because Annas served first

---

1. Mason, *Josephus and the New Testament*, 129.

during that year. The order Luke gives us is sequential, not authoritative.

As the evidence will show, this dynamic was more commonplace than one might think. The structure of the high-priestly office in the first century had actually become quite transient and corrupt—far more so than the text of the New Testament expresses.

Beginning with Valerius Gratus and continuing throughout at least Pilate's administration, we have enough examples to demonstrate that the office of the high priest had become an annually appointed office. Gratus, during his first four years, replaced four high priests in succession.[1] It was an especially Roman approach to government, mirroring the single-year terms found in offices like that of the *cursus honorum*, the Consul, Praetor, Aedile, and Quaestor, and likely many lower offices and magistracies as well. The fourth of Gratus' appointments, Caiaphas, at least according to Josephus' testimony, appears to have held the office for many successive years following that, with the implication from some obscure references that Gratus was essentially taking bribes from men who sought the position, thereby facilitating this extended tenure, in addition to Caiaphas allegedly having Herod Antipas as a patron.[2] Evidence of systemic corruption among Roman governors is plainly documented as early as Gratus and Pilate, and extended at least as late as Felix, who repeatedly attempted to extract money even from Paul, and Albinus, who accepted bribes to release people from prison.[3] D. R. Catchpole, in fact, suggested that, "for the long overlap" of Caiaphas' and Pilate's "respective official tenures," it should be, "attributed [...] more probably to Caiaphas's ability to pay for the office."[4]

The Talmud explicitly corroborates the practice, noting a period when "money was being paid for the purpose of obtaining the position of high priest," and that they "were changed every twelve months."[5] While the Talmud does not directly specify the timeframe, the stated parameters—bribery and annual turnover—did not exist until the

---

1. Joseph. *AJ* 18.33–35.

2. Eisler, *The Messiah Jesus and John the Baptist*, 18, 599; Hieron. *Comm. Matt.* 223 (Vallarsi, *PL* 26:201).

3. Philo *Leg.* 302; Acts 24:26; Joseph. *AJ* 20.215.

4. Catchpole, *Trial of Jesus*, 249; cf. Eisler, *The Messiah Jesus and John the Baptist*, 18–19.

5. bYoma 8b; Gill, *Exposition of the New Testament*, 1:484a.

Roman annexation. High priests during the Second Temple period served for life, and often considerably longer than a year, barring death, defilement, mutilation, or other disqualifying issues.[1] Although the practice of lifelong incumbency ended when Herod assumed the authority to appoint the high priests, the appointments under Herod and Archelaus were periodic—typically for political or judicial purposes—and the high-priestly position was rarely limited to a single year, absent some form of malfeasance.[2] We do not see any hint of rapid, annual turnover until Gratus, and, as already noted, it is also hinted that he was corrupt and accepting bribes, demonstrating that the Roman-occupation period beginning with Gratus was the unquestionable timeframe to which the Talmudic tradition refers.[3]

John likewise confirms the practice of an annual high priesthood and its continuation clear into the year of the crucifixion. Although the reference is subtle, John states on three separate occasions that Caiaphas was the "high priest that same year," with the Greek being τοῦ ἐνιαυτοῦ ἐκείνου in the genitive, "high priest of that year," or more succinctly, "that year's high priest."[4] Had John intended to say that Caiaphas was merely the high priest during that year, as the typical translation often portrays, the phrase would have more rightly been ἀρχιερεὺς ἐν τῷ ἐνιαυτῷ ἐκείνῳ or ἀρχιερεὺς τῷ ἐνιαυτῷ ἐκείνῳ. Instead, he deliberately uses the genitive, which creates a possessive—or attributive—relationship, suggesting that Caiaphas

---

1. Lev. 21:16–23; bYoma 12a–13a; Joseph. *AJ* 14.366, 17.165–166; Joseph. *BJ* 1.270.

2. Joseph. *AJ* 20.247–249. Herod appointed the obscure priest Ananelus to secure his government (Joseph. *AJ* 15.22). He appointed Aristobulus to appease Alexandra and Mariamne, who were making innovations to go to Antony over the indignity of Aristobulus being passed over for the high priesthood (Joseph. *AJ* 15.23–41). He appointed Simon, son of Boethus, in order to elevate Simon's social standing so he could marry his daughter (Joseph. *AJ* 15.320–322). He replaced Simon because he believed his wife Mariamne, Simon's daughter (Joseph. *AJ* 18.136; Joseph. *BJ* 1.562, 599), had conspired with Antipater to murder him (Joseph. *AJ* 17.78). He replaced Matthias for his complicity in the disruptions that resulted in the golden eagle being torn down (Joseph. *AJ* 17.164). Joazar was then removed by Archelaus on suspicion of his complicity in the uprising that had occurred during his absence to Rome after Herod's death (Joseph. *AJ* 17.339).

3. Joseph. *AJ* 18.33–35; Eisler, *The Messiah Jesus and John the Baptist*, 18, 599.

4. Jn. 11:49, 11:51, 18:13.

belonged to that specific year, not that he was merely serving coincident to it.

The peculiar phraseology is too blatant to be an accident. John added, "of that year" because the high priesthood, as stated in the Talmud, had become an annual office. Caiaphas was *that year's high priest*. And truth be told, this is not new information, even if it is somewhat obscure in the mainstream. John's particular phraseology and the implication of an annual office obtained through bribery have been recognized for centuries.[1] Steve Mason, though he struggles with the idea due to Caiaphas' accepted tenure of office, readily recognizes the implications of John's repeated statement, plainly asserting that, "John makes Caiaphas an annually appointed high priest ..." Eisler concluded the same, though with more conviction to the fact of the matter.[2]

In light of this information, the circumstance of Annas being titled high priest in Acts 4:6 loses all of its mystery. *Annas* was now the high priest, not Caiaphas, with Caiaphas notably absent the title and reduced to being merely "of high-priestly lineage"—a reversal of their earlier designations when Caiaphas held the office and Annas was identified as nothing more than the father-in-law of Caiaphas. We need not speculate about honorific titles, behind-the-scenes authority, or the public perception of an ex-Roman appointee. Annas was simply that year's administratively appointed high priest, just as Caiaphas had been in the previous administrative year. This, furthermore, provides us with the mechanism by which we find Caiaphas back in the position of high priest at the time of his dismissal by Vitellius. An additional rotation in incumbency clearly took place during the intervening years prior to 37 CE.

Recognition of this conspicuous fact—of a formal change in incumbency from Caiaphas to Annas—has simply gone unrealized in the shadow of the "high priest in principle" point of view. As already expressed, had it been any other high priest besides Annas—like Ananias, Theophilus, Simon Cantheras, etc.—no one would have ever questioned for even a moment that a change in the office had occurred. It is solely due to the perception that Annas and Caiaphas were

---

1. Gill, *Exposition of the New Testament*, 1:483b–484a.

2. Mason, *Josephus and the New Testament*, 130–131; Eisler, *The Messiah Jesus and John the Baptist*, 18–19.

simultaneously the high priest that this is viewed as anything other than what it was.

It is a fact, not an opinion, that in the months preceding Nisan of the crucifixion year, Caiaphas was "that year's high priest."[1] In Nisan of the following Jewish year, at the interrogation and trial of Jesus the night before his crucifixion, Caiaphas was "that year's high priest."[2] Then, about a month or so after Pentecost of the crucifixion year, *Annas* was the high priest, while Caiaphas was noticeably absent the title himself.[3] The texts do not indicate that they were both the high priest. To the contrary, in each case, one man holds the title while the other clearly does not. If one can divorce themselves from the unsubstantiated idea of a de jure/de facto high priesthood, which the evidence does not actually support, we have blatant proof of a transient office, with a shift in incumbency occurring in this particular year around late spring or early summer, when the office changed hands from Caiaphas to Annas.

And as we delve into the dynamics of the political climate in which this change in incumbency occurred, it becomes clear that the transition actually occurred right about where we would expect it to have happened.

Pontius Pilate, the Roman government official at the time in question, would have officiated Roman matters according to Roman protocols—a principle amply demonstrated by several of his actions during his tenure, such as the construction of an aqueduct to improve irrigation and water supply, or the provocative placement of Caesar's images in Jerusalem.[4] Given his notoriously inflexible disposition, there is not much room to argue this point.[5] His administrative habits, just like his public works and demonstrations of fidelity to the Emperor, would have been distinctly Roman and unaccommodating to Jewish sensibilities, as many of his overtly callous acts demonstrate.

Operating under this reality, the priestly aristocracy, which conducted itself as an autonomous civil and judicial governing body,

---

1. Jn. 11:47–54.

2. Jn. 18:13–24.

3. Acts 4:6.

4. Joseph. *AJ* 18.55–56, 60; Joseph. *BJ* 2.175, 169.

5. Philo *Leg.* 301.

complete with a council and several courts of law, was functionally analogous to the *boulai* that governed many Greek provincial cities.[1] The Romans routinely assimilated municipal bodies of this sort into their own administrative models, and indeed did so here as well, readily evidenced by Quirinius assuming control of the high offices and removing Joazar from the high priesthood upon Judaea's annexation.[2] With their local governing body, in fact, assimilated into the standard Roman administrative model, Pilate, later being the local ranking Roman official, would have controlled the local magistracies, including and especially the high-priestly appointments, as we also see to be the case with many of the governors throughout the greater part of the first century before the temple's destruction.[3]

Synchronizing the high-priestly appointments to his own administrative year would have been second nature—a natural and efficient solution to coordinate the various offices he had to manage. Although the high priesthood was Jewish in function, it was entirely subject to the Roman Praefect. It would have followed whatever administrative schedule he deemed appropriate. For the Judaean governors, that schedule would have been the provincial military schedule.

Historically, a *provincia* was not so much a place as it was a military post, and this is an important distinction to recognize. Men like Pontius Pilate weren't merely governors. They were military men, sent to oversee military endeavors. What made the "provinces" territorial as we understand them today was that fixed *provinciae* were ongoing military tasks, so they tended to remain focused on a specific region that needed continued military oversight.[4] Pilate wasn't precisely the governor of the province of Judaea in a territorial sense. Rather, he was a Praefect over the *provincia* assignment *in* Judaea, responsible, according to his post, for maintaining peace in the region against sedition, and to protect Rome's interests, since Palestine was pivotal to Mediterranean trade.

---

1. Mosaic law and the interpretations therefrom are comprehensive, covering both religious and civil law, from sacrifice protocols to judging disputes between neighbors over an ox fallen into a ditch on someone else's property.

2. Bowman, *Town Councils of Roman Egypt*, 8, 16; Dio Cass. 54.17.3; *P. Ryl.* 77; Joseph. *AJ* 18.3.

3. Joseph. *AJ* 20.249, 18.26, 34–35, 89, 123.

4. Drogula, *Commanders & Command*, 246.

These Roman provincial assignments tended to revolve around a summer schedule. Travel patterns and Roman law clarify when governors actually entered their provinces, with Claudius' edict being perhaps the clearest evidence. To combat what had become routine procrastination among those assigned to the provinces, Claudius decreed that they had to depart for their provinces by April 1st.[1] Relative to the three-month travel limitation established in the time of Augustus for officers dismissed from their province to return to Rome, Claudius' choice of April 1st is somewhat telling.[2]

Real-world examples show that Cicero departed for his province on May 10th and arrived on July 31st.[3] This was just shy of three months, a journey consistent in duration with the three-month travel limitation, showing that the three-month deadline was based on known travel times. Cicero, in fact, was deliberately slow in reaching his province, since he had no desire to be there. Some provinces might have been reached sooner, others later. However, as a working allowance, three months became the standard for travel, at least for the return journey. So, when we consider a plausible and established expectation of three months to return from a province, and by default a similarly inferable expectation to arrive at one, when Claudius imposed a strict departure deadline of April 1st, it seems clear to me that provincial governors were expected to arrive and take up their posts no later than the 1st of July. I am confident that Claudius did not select April 1st arbitrarily. It was based on an established target date. This is no different from the experience of every working person today. If you know you need to be at work by 7:00 a.m., you leave by 6:30 if it will take you 20–30 minutes to get there. If you know you have to leave by 6:30 to get to work on time, you set your alarm for 5:30 if you know it will take you an hour to shower, get dressed, and eat breakfast. This is not rocket science. They knew it could take up to three months to reach a province, so Claudius set a departure date commensurate with the expected travel.

Consistent with this, March 23rd marked the beginning of the campaign season, celebrated as the *Tubilustrium*, directly associated

---

1. Dio Cass. 60.11.6.

2. Dio Cass. 53.15.6.

3. Cic. *Att.* 5.2, 5.15.

with Mars in the March observance.[1] The legions marched out for the summer campaigns shortly after this festival, placing them ideally at their intended destinations around the beginning of the summer, when campaigns were historically conducted, corroborating an approximate July 1st starting point, which is not long after the official start of summer.

The timing is further evidenced in the case of Coponius. He returned to Rome a "little after" an incident that happened during the Feast of Unleavened Bread, when he was succeeded by Marcus Ambivius.[2] Depending on precisely how long "a little after" happened to be, which is a purely subjective exercise interpretively, we have at the very least evidence of a provincial succession following the Passover, and realistically late spring or early summer if Ambivius left Rome in or after April, which would have put him in Judaea at the earliest by the middle of June.

When we consider these multiple lines of evidence, we can confidently deduce that military *provinciae* were entered upon in the late spring or early summer. The documented convergence of summer campaigns, travel patterns, the travel allowance, and Claudius' calculated departure deadline all point toward July 1st as a probable target date for provincial succession. Although we are not fortunate enough to have a direct statement to confirm it definitively, the evidence in general is sufficient to conclusively demonstrate, at the very least, that provincial assignments were entered upon in the late spring or early summer, if not on July 1st itself.

In light of all this, let me reiterate that Pilate operated on an administrative cycle that synchronized with the military season, as discussed, with the evidence strongly pointing to a July-to-July

---

1. Fowler, *Religious Experience of the Roman People*, 96–97; Scullard, *Festivals and Ceremonies of the Roman Republic*, 195; Beard, North, and Price, *Religions of Rome*, 1:43; Balsdon, *Life and Leisure in Ancient Rome*, 70; Ov. *Fast.* 3.849–50; Fasti Praenestini, *CIL* 1² : 234, Mar. 23. "Feriae Marti hic · dies appellatur · ita · quod in atrio sutorio tubi lustrantur quibus in sacris utuntur · Lutatius ovidem · Clavam eam ait esse in ruina palati incense a Gallis repertam qua Romulus urbem inauguraverit"—"This day is called the festival of Mars...." cf. Fasti Caeretani, *CIL* 1² : 212, Mar. 23; Fasti Maffeiani, *CIL* 1² : 223, Mar. 23; Fasti Pavlini et Vaticani, *CIL* 1² : 242, Mar. 23; Fasti Farnesiani, *CIL* 1² : 250, Mar. 23.

2. Joseph. *AJ* 18.30–31.

administrative year. It is logically probable that Pilate, as well as his predecessors, synchronized the local municipal offices to this same schedule, if for no other reason than efficiency and simplicity.

This being the case, the transition from Caiaphas to Annas a month or so after Pentecost, as stated, is about where we would expect to see the office change hands while under a Roman official and subject to his scheduling prerogatives. The timing of the transition itself testifies to the reality of the scheduling assimilation. A transition in late spring or early summer would have been perfectly harmonious with the administrative cycle of a provincial Praefect overseeing a local government office under Roman control.

Further examples can also be detected. In a scenario similar to that of Caiaphas and Annas in Acts 4:6, the chain of events at the beginning of 37 CE reveals a similar story and pattern. Following Pilate's dismissal by Vitellius around January of 37 CE, Vitellius arrived in Jerusalem for Passover.[1] He removed Caiaphas from the high priesthood and conferred it on Jonathan.[2] But barely two months later, Vitellius returned during another major festival of the Jews, presumably Pentecost, which, similar to the crucifixion year, fell on or about June 9th in this instance.[3] During the three days he was there, Vitellius removed Jonathan from the high priesthood and bestowed it on Theophilus, with no indication that Jonathan had done anything worthy of being removed after such a brief term.[4] Later interactions show that Jonathan was esteemed an honorable person worthy of the dignity,

---

1. Joseph. *AJ* 18.89–90. The timing of Pilate's dismissal is directly relative to the three-month return statute and Tiberius' death on March 16th of 37 CE, prior to Pilate reaching Rome. By these parameters, Pilate could not have been dismissed much earlier than January of 37 CE.

2. Joseph. *AJ* 18.95.

3. Joseph. AJ 18.122, 124. That this second festival, although unnamed, was likely Pentecost can be confirmed both by the news arriving of Tiberius' death—which rules out later festivals—as well as the strict interval count of Caligula's reign, who reigned four years, less four months (Joseph. *AJ* 19.201), and/or three years and eight months (Joseph. *BJ* 2.204). Caligula died in the month Shebat. The interval from Shebat to Sivan is four months. The interval from Sivan to Shebat is eight months.

4. Joseph. *AJ* 18.123.

and that he even held the position again from 52–54 CE, despite refusing it when offered it by Agrippa more than a decade prior.[1]

Although it is a circumstantial inference, I strongly suspect that Caiaphas had been removed unseasonably for some malfeasance, and that Jonathan was the chosen replacement to finish out the remainder of that high-priestly administrative year. Meanwhile, given the temporary absence of a regular Praefect with Pilate having been relieved of duty, when Vitellius returned in the vicinity of June, he expeditiously handled the annual appointment himself while he was there, appointing Theophilus to succeed Jonathan on the appropriate date for the change in office.[2]

While R. A. Horsley debates the many speculations concerning why Jonathan was removed, whether he was too much of a Roman sympathizer, or perhaps because Theophilus was "a wiser choice for High Priest in the circumstances," the timing of this change in the high priesthood is too coincidental to ignore.[3] What we have here is another demonstrable transition of the high priests at almost precisely the same time of year, and in perfect alignment with the predictive cycle one would expect while operating within a Roman provincial schedule.

Overall, the pattern is consistent. We have at least two examples up to this point of high-priestly transitions occurring in late spring or early summer, which are notably synchronized with what we know of the Roman provincial schedule.

---

1. Joseph. *AJ* 19.313–316. Jonathan's refusal to take the office from Agrippa was ethical. It was not that he rejected the high priesthood or would not accept it again, as he clearly did. He just did not want it the way he was being gifted it—"I am satisfied with having once put on the sacred garments; for I then put them on after a more holy manner than I should now receive them again" (Joseph. *AJ* 19.314). The implication is actually in line with the premise of this work, showing that Jonathan had no interest in the position when acquired by unethical means (i.e. bribery, political favors, etc.).

2. Joseph. *AJ* 18.123. Vitellius did send Marcellus to "take care of the affairs of Judea" (Joseph. *AJ* 18.89), but there is no indication that he was a proper Praefect. He is mentioned as an ἐπιμελητής (an overseer, manager, or caretaker), not a ἡγεμών (governor). He merely filled the gap between Pilate and Agrippa I to provide some form of Roman oversight.

3. Horsley, "High Priests," *JSJ* 17, no. 1 (1986): 37–38.

When we follow along the same logical precedent, Luke 3:2 very suddenly becomes perfectly intelligible. What we are looking at are overlapping annual systems. During the specific Jewish year in question, Annas and Caiaphas were both the high priest. The first of the two, Annas, was high priest from the summer of the previous Jewish year through the summer of that current year. Then the office changed hands to Caiaphas, who served in the office for the remainder of that Jewish year and into the next.

Jewish Year	Tib. 14	Tib. 15	
Roman Administrative Year	Annas		Caiaphas
Julian Year	28 CE		

This also sheds some light on Luke's long-contemplated use of the singular ἀρχιερέως rather than the plural ἀρχιερεῖς when referring to both Annas and Caiaphas as the high priest, the peculiarity of which has been debated by scholars for centuries. The singular implies a single office shared by two men, which is the root problem that has led to interpretations like the de jure/de facto power dynamic, or in some cases, the idea that the two men took turns officiating throughout the year, like Roman consuls passing the *fasces* of *imperium domi* once a month.[1] Others, like McEachern, say that "Luke's use of the singular *archiereōs* (3:2) 'rightly suggests that there could only be one high-priest, but the combination of the two names is strange,'" ultimately concluding that Luke simply did not know which man was the high priest.[2] Suffice it to say, it is not a new problem linguistically. Scholars have debated Luke's choice of the singular for quite some time. From one commentator to the next, they have simply been unable to make any logical sense of it, because, culturally and legally, two men having the title of high priest at the same time simply is not credible, which is what makes the "high priest behind the scenes" so appealing. It allows two men to serve as the high priest simultaneously without

---

1. Gill, *Exposition of the New Testament*, 484a; Henry, *Commentary*, 611; Clarke, *New Testament*, on Luke 3:2; Dion. Hal. 5.2.1.

2. McEachern, "Dual Witness and Sabbath Motif," *CJT* 12 (1966): 268. McEachern's in-line quote is from Creed, *Gospel According to St. Luke*, 49; cf. Wolter, *The Gospel According to Luke*, 1:159; Mason, *Josephus and the New Testament*, 130.

assigning the official title to more than one man.

However, when we evaluate this problem relative to the solution offered, which is to say that the high-priestly administrative year divided the standard calendar year, the practical result would have been two men each holding the singular office of the high priesthood within the space of a Jewish year. Luke is writing within the context of the fifteenth year of Tiberius. If one man held the high priesthood for part of that year, and the other held it for the other part of that year, then the calendar year, divided between the two, would be the year of the high priesthood of Annas, and the year of the high priesthood of Caiaphas, which the Greek structure technically represents.[1] This is precisely what Luke's singular construction expresses. The office itself remained singular, even though it passed from one man to the other within the span of that single year. In a manner of speaking, although the alternation theory never truly took root, it would appear that those advocating it were closer to the truth than most realize. This really was similar in a sense to the Roman consuls passing the *fasces*, but rather than a monthly or other irregular alternation, it simply shifted definitively from one to the other mid-year.

The Administrative Continuity Objection

---

1. The construction ἐπὶ ἀρχιερέως Ἅννα καὶ Καϊάφα employs distributed coordination, where the genitive relationship established by ἀρχιερέως is distributed across both names via the conjunction καί. The proper names Ἅννα and Καϊάφα appear in the genitive case because they stand in both appositional relation to ἀρχιερέως (identifying who the high priest is) and possessive relation to the office itself (whose high priesthood it was). Just as the English construction, "Robert gave presents to you and me," distributes the prepositional relationship ("to you" and "to me") without explicit repetition, Luke's singular ἀρχιερέως governs both Annas and Caiaphas individually: "in the high priesthood of Annas" and "[in the high priesthood] of Caiaphas." While this expanded form is not how the passage is *translated* word-for-word—the repetition, much like the definite article in many cases, is not explicitly represented in English—the dual relationship is nevertheless implicit in the grammatical structure. The names are genitive due to case agreement with ἀρχιερέως (appositional function), but the case agreement is itself the grammatical mechanism by which Greek expresses the possessive relationship. The structure does not require explicit repetition to convey the dual relationship. The high priesthood belonged to both men separately and individually.

About the only real objection that can be made to any of this would be the inference of administrative continuity for each high priest in Josephus' narrative. In other words, Josephus appears to record uninterrupted periods of administration for the high priests, as we have already briefly touched on concerning Caiaphas. The one recorded as appointed is always the one recorded as removed, with no obvious evidence of other high priests rotating in or out during these periods. If there were, indeed, a rotation in the office, one would expect, at least occasionally, to hear of another high priest within the confines of another's administration. That this never overtly occurs strongly suggests that Josephus, himself a priest contemporary to the era, was recording uninterrupted administrations with no knowledge of other high priests serving rotations during any of these periods.

And this is a fair perspective to consider. It is this very thing that Steve Mason noted concerning the clear language in John. He ultimately acknowledges John's intent that it was an annual office, but denies the fact of it based on Caiaphas' extended linear tenure, stating:

> John repeatedly identifies Caiaphas as "high priest that year" (11:51; 18:13). A non-Jewish reader would presumably infer that the Jewish high priest, like many others in the Greco-Roman world, was annually elected as a civic official. Even though the high priesthood had lost its life-long tenure by Jesus' time, however, it was by no means an annual position. According to Josephus, Caiaphas held it for about eighteen years.[1]

If we look at Josephus, he tells us, just as one set of examples, that Agrippa replaced Matthias with Elioneus, son of Cantheras. Herod of Chalcis then removed Elioneus and appointed Joseph, son of Camydus. Later, when Cumanus replaced Tiberius Alexander as the governor of Judaea, Herod removed Joseph and appointed Ananias, son of Nebedeu.[2] In each case, one man, one period of administration, and no direct mention of anyone appointed in between. This is precisely the narrative framework described in the objection. If

---

1. Mason, *Josephus and the New Testament*, 130–131.

2. Joseph. *AJ* 19.342, 20.16, 20.103.

there was a rotation of some sort, where is the evidence of interruption in these linear administrative patterns?

The evidence, in a word, is Ismael. Outside of the running narrative, Josephus casually comments in an unrelated section of his history that, "a little before the beginning of this war, when Claudius was emperor of the Romans, and Ismael was our high priest, and when so great a famine was come upon us," substantial quantities of flour were brought into the temple at the feast of unleavened bread.[1]

This famine occurred during the governance of the two procurators Fadus and Tiberius Alexander, beginning prior to 47 CE and extending at least into 51 CE, according to Tacitus' account of Rome suffering from the same famine, no doubt a repercussive effect of other regional famines that made grain generally scarce throughout the Mediterranean.[2] During this period, we have the previously mentioned documented successions of high priests. Elioneus, son of Cantheras, was replaced by Joseph, son of Camydus in 43 CE.[3] He was succeeded by Ananias, son of Nebedeus, appointed by Herod of Chalcis in 47 CE during the eighth year of Claudius, right around the time Cumanus arrived to succeed Tiberius Alexander.[4] Ananias demonstrably continued in office at least until 52 CE—the twelfth year of Claudius—when he was sent to Rome.[5] Yet, Josephus identifies Ismael—not Elioneus, Joseph, or Ananias—as "our high priest" during this famine period.[6]

The only documented record of Ismael being appointed high priest is after the death of Jonathan in 54 CE, with no mention of who he replaced specifically.[7] The inference from Josephus' narrative would be that it was Jonathan, though we know from Acts that Ananias was the high priest around Pentecost of 54 CE, some months after Jonathan's death.[8] There is simply no record of Ismael being

---

1. Joseph. *AJ* 3.320–321.

2. Joseph. *AJ* 20.97, 100–101; Tac. *Ann.* 12.41, 43; cf. Oros. 7.6; Acts 11:28.

3. Joseph. *AJ* 19.342.

4. Joseph. *AJ* 20.103–104.

5. Joseph. *AJ* 20.162.

6. Joseph. *AJ* 3.320–321.

7. Joseph. *AJ* 20.131, 179; Joseph. *BJ* 2.243.

8. Porcius Festus succeeded Marcus Antonius Felix in the summer of 55 CE, though some erroneously date it later, ranging between 56 CE and 59 CE. We know that when Felix

appointed during these famine years. Neither is there a record of Elioneus, Joseph, or Ananias being temporarily removed to accommodate him. Ismael is declared the high priest during a year—or a span of years—that Josephus elsewhere attributes entirely to the seemingly continuous and unbroken administrations of one or more of these other high priests.

So, despite how it may appear, the notion that these high priests enjoyed uninterrupted tenures is demonstrably false.

Not only do we have the example of Ismael. We also have Jonathan. Josephus' record shows the appointment of Ananias, and then documents the appointment of Ismael.[1] But we have no record of Jonathan being appointed, though he is blatantly named the high priest and described as vexatious to Felix, which exemplifies his position of authority.[2] We have to extrapolate his appointment from the context. Ananias was sent to Rome right around the twelfth year of Claudius' reign to answer to charges laid against him, though Ananias clearly

---

returned to Rome, some prominent Jews had brought charges against him before Caesar. It was only via his brother, Pallas, that Felix avoided punishment (Joseph. *AJ* 20.182). Pallas, at that time, held a place of honor in Nero's court, and is said to have practically controlled the monarchy (Joseph. *AJ* 20.182; Tac. *Ann.* 13.14). But this authority was extremely short-lived. Seneca and Burrus, disapproving of Pallas' "vulgar and objectionable" association with Agrippina, Nero's mother, plotted to remove Pallas from favor (Dio Cass. 61.3.2–3). As a result of their efforts, Nero and Pallas had a falling out shortly before the December 17th Saturnalia of 55 CE, with sarcastic and bitter words exchanged (Tac. *Ann.* 13.11, 14, 15, 24). For Felix to have received aid from Pallas in Nero's court, his departure from Jerusalem had to precede December of 55 CE. Pallas was irrevocably *persona non grata* beyond that point. That puts Felix's departure very solidly in the summer of 55 CE, with Paul's journey to Rome shortly thereafter, near the fast on the 10th of Tishri (Acts 27:9; Lev. 23:27–28), which fell around September 21st that year. With Paul's return to Judaea in the late spring of 54 CE, and Felix's departure in the summer of 55 CE, the two years Paul spent in Felix's custody are the two inclusive calendar years 54 CE and 55 CE. That definitively determines Ananias as the high priest at Pentecost in 54 CE.

1. Joseph. *AJ* 20.103, 179.
2. Joseph. *AJ* 20.162.

regained the high priesthood at some point following his return, since Paul finds himself on trial before Ananias around Pentecost of 54 CE.[1]

The specifics of when and how Jonathan received the high priesthood are unclear. With Ananias having been sent to Rome, someone had to step into that role. The position couldn't be left unattended. It is possible that Jonathan simply filled the vacancy in his absence. However, we do have a potentially conflicting report in *Wars*, suggesting that Jonathan actually went with Ananias to Rome. This sort of scenario could indicate that Ananias had been removed from authority and that Jonathan had been appointed high priest in his stead, perhaps even by Claudius himself.[2] However, the pairing of Ananias and Jonathan in later contexts, after the death of this Jonathan, suggests that a different Jonathan attended Ananias to Rome.[3] Whatever the case, by the time Felix came as the governor of Judaea, appointed per Jonathan's direct solicitation on his behalf, Jonathan was the high priest, and both his ability to influence the emperor concerning the appointment of a governor, and his later vexatious admonitions towards Felix, which would have been considered impudence from a man of lesser status, demonstrate his formal position.[4]

By all accounts, Jonathan was the high priest beginning at some point in 52 CE, following Ananias being sent to Rome. He remained high priest until his assassination early in 54 CE, in the first year of Nero.[5] We know that his death was early in the year because it preceded the Egyptian rebel, whose uprising, in turn, predated Pentecost and Paul's trial, at which time Ananias was back in the position of

---

1. Acts 23:1–10; Joseph. *AJ* 20.131, 138.

2. Joseph. *BJ* 2.243.

3. Joseph. *Vit.* 39, 61, 64.

4. Joseph. *AJ* 20.162.

5. Joseph. *AJ* 20.158, 162, 164, 169–172; bRosh Hash. 2a–b. The legal designation of a king to a year in a formal sense belonged to the succeeding king, except in the case of successions in Nisan and Adar, which could be counted as belonging to either. While it is common modern practice to count Nero's reign beginning by direct succession from the death of Claudius on October 13th of 54 CE, it would be properly counted from Nisan of that year by Jewish reckoning. Although Claudius was still technically alive and in power when the event of the Egyptian occurred, the history retrospectively designates the event in Nero's legal first year of reign, which ran from Nisan 1 of 54 CE to Nisan 1 of 55 CE. The time of Paul's trial, and the succession from Felix to Festus, further bears this out.

high priest, and the Egyptian was still in recent enough memory that Claudius Lysias, the chief captain, thought Paul was he.[1] The events are all very closely related.

Nevertheless, Josephus neglects to mention Jonathan's appointment, as well as Ananias' reappointment.

Interestingly enough, when you carefully consider the particulars of the transitions in this scenario, you will find that it is actually another obvious example of a circumstance like that of Caiaphas, where he was removed prematurely, replaced with a substitute to finish out the administrative year, who was then himself replaced in turn at the time of the annual rotation. In this instance, Jonathan was the high priest. He was murdered while in office, leaving the high priesthood vacant prematurely. A replacement, Ananias, stepped in to finish out the administrative year—during which time Paul ended up on trial—and at the proper transition season, Ananias was removed, and Ismael was appointed in his place.

Another example of an undocumented high priesthood is that of Ananus in late 67 CE. Ananus is called the high priest, and said in a speech to the people that he was "clothed with the vestments of the high priesthood" and "called by that most venerable name," though there is no record of Ananus having been appointed anywhere in the proximity of the high priesthoods of either Matthias or Phannias, the former being the last legitimate high priest appointment recorded, and the latter the documented puppet high priest appointed by the rebel faction.[2] Only the actual high priest himself wore the vestments.[3] Ananus was *the* high priest, not just an aristocrat in this instance, acting on some honorary title. Yet … no record of his appointment, nor the deposition of Matthias.

So, it needs to be recognized that not all of Josephus' examples are rigidly structured with absolute unbroken continuity. While his narrative may habitually represent the perception of one man, one term, and no interruptions, it actually turns out that this is not strictly accurate, as the examples of Jonathan, Ismael, and Ananus all adequately demonstrate, further corroborated by Ananias in Acts, and the

---

1. Acts 21:38.

2. Joseph. *Vit.* 193–194; Joseph. *BJ* 4.155–156, 162–164, 318; Joseph. *AJ* 20.223.

3. Joseph. *AJ* 3.191, 15.403; Exod. 28:1–4, 29:29–30.

unmistakable shifts between Caiaphas and Annas in the Gospels. The administrative continuity pattern that appears so conclusive—wherein the one appointed is invariably the one removed—creating the illusion of unbroken administrations, is sincerely the coincidence it appears to be. It only *looks* like the terms are unbroken successions.

In reality, as shown, we have evidence that some of them were, in fact, interrupted administrations, despite the same man holding the high seat at both the beginning and end of a given range of years. What creates the illusion of continuity are the mechanisms by which the annual appointments were both acquired and retained. Politics, patronage, and bribery.

Simply put, if the office was annual and obtained through bribery, which the evidence says was the case on both accounts, then it has to be logically assumed that the person or family possessing the sufficient wealth to secure the office in the first place was likewise of sufficient wealth to retain the office year after year. I would even suggest that by currying favor with the king or governor in charge of the appointments, the bribes may have become something of a formal arrangement. It would give the king or governor surety of a steady annual supply of personal revenue off the books, and it would give the high priest of the arrangement peace of mind, knowing he would not have to fight tooth and nail each year.

This is the perspective taken by Eisler.

> Evidently a one-year term of office had become the rule since Gratus, and Caiaphas' long term, lasting throughout the administration of Pilate, is to be explained on the basis of a personal understanding he had with the latter, which means, that he paid him annually a bribe as high as or higher than that which any of his rival candidates could afford. Since Josephus reports the removal of Caiaphas through Vitellius as late as *Ant.* xviii. S 95, it follows that this high priest did indeed, as Jerome states after Josephus, buy his office from year to year by paying Herod (above, p. 18 n. 1) and, obviously, also the Roman governor, who had the right of veto.[1]

It can be speculated that on occasion, a rival might offer a significantly better bribe, which was to the king's or the governor's benefit,

---

1. Eisler, *The Messiah Jesus and John the Baptist*, 18–19.

not only in the immediate monetary sense, but also as a bargaining tool. A higher offer from a rival would give the king or governor an excuse to renegotiate—or extort—a higher bribe arrangement from the ousted high priest. And as would be expected in a corrupt and volatile political environment, the king or governor's demands would be met.

In some instances, especially within specific families, and particularly in the case of Annas and Caiaphas, the alternation we observe may very well have been deliberately planned and internally consensual within the family group. If the annual bribe was supplied by the family in general, it stands to reason that family members would be in the rotation. I anticipate this would have been the case for any of the prominent families, though I can only speculate relative to the evidence.

Whatever the case, we are talking about acquisition and retention through bribery, which is specifically what the Talmud records— "money was being paid for the purpose of obtaining the position of high priest, and the [high priests] were changed every twelve months." So, when Josephus reports the same high priest being appointed and then deposed, the true and substantiated explanation is that the same man did, in many cases, retain the office throughout that span of years through consistent bribery. An annual appointment does not necessarily indicate a change in the high priest. It just means he had to gain the seat year after year, much as Augustus held the annual consulship for eight years in a row at one point.[1]

In most cases, when we read about specifically recorded depositions—this one was removed and that one appointed—what we are actually witnessing is external administrative oversight outside the norm. We do have evidence that the priests, to a degree, were permitted some amount of self-governance. Josephus stated that, "Some of these were the political governors of the people under the reign of Herod, and under the reign of Archelaus his son, although, after their death, the government became an aristocracy, and the high priests were intrusted with a dominion over the nation."[2] On at least two occasions, in fact, government interference actually provoked unrest

---

1. Suet. *Aug.* 26.2.

2. Joseph. *AJ* 20.251.

and infighting.[1] Barring a few very select instances, Josephus is not talking about the regular cycles or rotation. He is talking about outside government interference and the removal of an individual entirely from consideration for the post. It is like the difference between a manager assigning shifts and expecting everyone to work their schedule, versus terminating someone altogether.

Caiaphas, for example, retained the office from 20 CE to 37 CE, throughout the administrations of Gratus and Pilate, with a few abdications to Annas that we can document.[2] When Pilate was dismissed, and Vitellius visited Jerusalem, he removed Caiaphas completely. He was not simply changing the high priest in rotation. We never hear the name Caiaphas again after that point. He was permanently put to pasture. In agreement with this analysis of Caiaphas' circumstance, Schwartz says:

> For our part, however, we would suggest that Vitellius in fact fired Caiaphas at the same time he suspended Pilate, which would have been reasonable, given Caiaphas' long tenure and his association with Pilate.[3]

With Caiaphas so long in control and governors changing so rarely during the reign of Tiberius, the entire high-priestly caste would have been jockeying for position, well aware that, with Pilate gone and a new governor coming in, Caiaphas would at last be politically vulnerable.[4] They would have made every effort to curry favor and disparage him to Vitellius. In turn, Vitellius, who had no intimate knowledge of Caiaphas, or any known relationship with him, nor any standing financial arrangement, had no reason to doubt or ignore allegations made by Caiaphas' opponents, nor any obligation or motivation to let him remain in power. In fact, as I already pointed out, he was removed from the high priesthood around the Passover, which was unseasonable and arbitrary. Acting as a responsible overseer in the absence of an assigned Praefect, he removed a presumably corrupt high priest and appointed a substitute to finish out the year. He then

---

1. Joseph. *AJ* 20.179–181, 213–214.

2. Lk. 3:2; Acts 4:6; Joseph. *AJ* 18.95.

3. Schwartz, *Jewish Background of Christianity*, 213.

4. Joseph. *AJ* 18.172–177; Tac. *Ann.* 1.80, 4.6.

later facilitated the annual rotation from Jonathan to Theophilus at the normal rotation period, about two months later. In this case, I have to agree with Schwartz that Caiaphas appears to have been removed for punitive reasons, vulnerable during a gubernatorial change, which is precisely the kind of circumstance we would expect rivals to exploit.

Many of Josephus' other examples demonstrate a similar character. The essential and perceivable pattern was that a given priest would essentially win favor, outbid his competition, establish a working relationship with the current governor or king, and serve more or less uninterrupted, barring the occasional hiccup with a rival outbidding him in a particular year. When a new governor arrived, that high priest had to fight with all of his rivals to retain or establish a working relationship with the new king or governor, though, as the record shows, they were often unsuccessful.

The hard changes—those that ended up being documented—tended to be made under extenuating circumstances or following a change in authority over the region. When Quirinius came, he removed Joazar. When Gratus came, he removed Annas. Relative to Annas being in office coming into 28 CE, it would appear that Pilate removed Caiaphas upon his arrival in 27 CE. When Pilate was later removed, and Vitellius came to Jerusalem, he removed Caiaphas. When Cumanus arrived, Herod of Chalcis had Joseph removed. At the time Felix came in Ananias' absence, Jonathan was appointed. A change in the governmental power dynamic essentially invalidated any standing arrangements that would have existed, financial or otherwise, stripping the current incumbent of any security they might have had. Some of the changes have the character of personal favors, especially under Agrippa and Herod of Chalcis. Some of them centered around accusations from rival factions concerning maladministration, abuse of power, or similar. Some appear to have been routine, like the transition from Jonathan to Theophilus. But most have a clear indication of some political motivation. The bottom line is that, in the vast majority of examples, there is a reason, overt or covert, behind the dismissal of one man and the appointment of the next.

Whatever the reason, men removed from the high priesthood were no longer in favor with the king or governor. Someone else had managed to secure that dignity. Continued appointment to the annual rotation, no matter the bribe, was difficult to achieve at that point. It was not *impossible*, but for them to gain a concession when they were *personae non gratae* would hardly have been an easy task. Practically speaking, once they were out, they were out, effectively ending their sequential incumbencies.

So, simply put, the person appointed tended to be the one who dominated the office during that period, which is why Josephus appears to list high priests with a sense of continuity. They obtained the position through bribery, patronage, and disparagement of their rivals, and they retained it by the same means. It was politics at its finest, and that game has not changed in two thousand years.

In which case, relative to the overall preponderance of evidence, this anticipated objection from Josephus, although meritorious, does not contradict the annual cycles, and the simple nature of politics and the documented corruption of the period very adequately demonstrates the mechanism by which this continuity pattern naturally manifested itself. Josephus does have unexplained gaps. His chronicle of the high priests is incomplete. There is evidence of anachronistic high priests mentioned during the alleged unbroken administrations of other high priests. On all points, the objection fails.

But to tie this all up with a nice, neat bow, we even have evidence in Josephus' own narrative testifying to the rotation system. Unfortunately, it is buried in the translation, so it goes entirely unnoticed.

While dealing with the history of the zealots who overran Jerusalem, Josephus notes at one point:

> Now the people were come to that degree of meanness and fear, and these robbers to that degree of madness, that these last took upon them to appoint high priests. So when they had disannulled the succession, according to those families out of which the high priests used to be made, they ordained certain unknown and ignoble persons for that office, that they might have their assistance in their wicked undertakings; for such as obtained this highest of all honors, without any desert, were forced to comply with those that bestowed it on them.[1]

Because Whiston's translation in this instance neglects some of the nuance, it is easy enough to miss the significance of the statement. What it *appears* to say is that the robbers were so presumptuous that

---

1. Joseph. *BJ* 4.147–149, Whiston edn.

they appointed high priests, which, by this overall translation, would seem to coordinate with the ignoble persons they ordained for that office, rather than individuals from the families of the succession.

However, to be precise about what is being said:

Συνέβη δὲ εἰς τοσοῦτον τὸν μὲν δῆμον ταπεινότητος καὶ δέους, ἐκείνους δὲ ἀπονοίας προελθεῖν, ὡς ἐπ᾽ αὐτοῖς εἶναι καὶ τὰς χειροτονίας τῶν ἀρχιερέων. ἄκυρα γοῦν τὰ γένη ποιήσαντες, ἐξ ὧν κατὰ διαδοχὰς οἱ ἀρχιερεῖς ἀπεδείκνυντο, καθίστασαν ἀσήμους καὶ ἀγενεῖς, ἵν᾽ ἔχοιεν συνεργοὺς τῶν ἀσεβημάτων: τοῖς γὰρ παρ᾽ ἀξίαν ἐπιτυχοῦσι τῆς ἀνωτάτω τιμῆς ὑπακούειν ἦν ἀνάγκη τοῖς παρασχοῦσι.

It happened that the people advanced to such a degree of meanness and fear, and those [robbers] to such madness, that even the appointments of the high priests came to be in their power. Having made invalid the families from which, according to the successions, the high priests were being appointed, they established unknown and ignoble persons, so that they might have collaborators in their impieties. For it was necessary for those who had obtained the highest honor beyond their worth to obey those who had provided it. (Joseph. *BJ* 4.147–149)

When you appropriately view this passage through the lens of a known system of annual high priests, it is plain as day what Josephus is saying here. While the Whiston and Loeb translations both alter the content to accommodate their interpretations of his meaning, understanding the true intent brings it all into sharp focus.

The zealots took control of the appointments—a plural noun, because the appointments were an annual and plural institution. The appointments were for high priests, plural, because each year had its own designated high priest (Jn. 11:49, 11:51, 18:13), even though it was often the same incumbent year after year. They disannulled the oligarchical families—the high-priestly caste we have already discussed—who were the aristocrats from whom the successions, plural, were being appointed, written here in the imperfect passive indicative, meaning a past-tense, habitual, or annual series of events that was ongoing. Everything about this passage is in perfect harmony with what has been described throughout the preceding arguments.

It is also worth noting, in conclusion to this continuity objection, that after a certain point Josephus stopped recording the specific lengths of the high-priestly careers, which is precisely what we would expect if they weren't remaining in office uninterrupted. He lists the lengths of service up through Hyrcanus, but gives none during the Roman period, not even for lengthy ones such as that of Caiaphas, whose tenure allegedly lasted about eighteen inclusive years.[1] The only Roman-era high priest whose precise term is mentioned is Ananus, son of Ananus, who was deposed after three months—yet Josephus notes this only because his removal was unseasonable, resulting from his presumptuous trial and execution of James, brother of Jesus.[2]

Conclusion

In the end, what we are ultimately looking at is a system of annual high priests whose appointments ran on an administrative year from approximately July to July, overlapping the Nisan-to-Nisan Jewish year. The office was held by members of a high-priestly aristocracy who obtained and held the office through bribery and patronage, typically for many years at a time, though not without the occasional documented interruption. Instances of infighting and unrest show that the sectarian and family rivalries were very real, and other examples of accusations and disparagement demonstrate political machinations, maneuvering, and manipulation.

This puzzle from Luke 3:2 has vexed scholars for at least the last three centuries that I can document, going back as far as John Gill's 1746 *Exposition of the New Testament*, where he wrestles with the problem of Luke's dual high priests. Even he notes that his own predecessors had correctly identified that the high priesthood had become venal, obtained through bribery, and that it changed hands annually, based on the same information provided here.[3] Yet, despite having all the key pieces of evidence at their disposal, we have made it to present day without anyone truly reconciling how both men could be called high priest at the same time without contradicting Jewish

---

1. Joseph. *AJ* 20.237–245.

2. Joseph. *AJ* 20.197–203.

3. Gill, *Exposition of the New Testament*, 483b.

law or custom, distorting historical reality, or altering the sense of Luke's statement to something other than what his words plainly say, which is itself ironic given the number of expositors who comment about the quality of Luke's Greek. We have discussed the various solutions that have been proposed: Annas retaining authority as a former high priest, *sagan* (deputy high priest), or even, implausibly, the *nasi*. But none of these arguments holds up under scrutiny.

The subtle clue scholars have persistently overlooked is the Roman authoritative priority. They assume a Jewish year for the high priesthood, which I concede is easy enough to do. But with a Roman governor assigning the appointments, the timing of the high-priestly office is subject to the whims of Roman procedure. The office was Jewish, but the scheduling was Roman. The mismatch between the Roman administrative cycle (July to July) and the Jewish calendar year (Nisan to Nisan) allows a single Jewish year to contain portions of two administrative cycles, and by extension, two different high-priestly appointments. That this is fact rather than speculation is clear enough in the blatant juxtaposition of John 18:13 and Acts 4:6. The high priesthood changed hands in the summer following Pentecost. Caiaphas was the high priest before Pentecost, and Annas was the high priest after Pentecost.

This is the circumstance of Luke 3:2, but in reverse. The Jewish year, identified by the regnal year of the reigning monarch—the fifteenth year of the reign of Tiberius Caesar—began with one high priest in power, Annas, who was then replaced by Caiaphas around July. Caiaphas then presumably retained the high priesthood until the administrative year overlapping the crucifixion, when he was replaced by Annas after Pentecost in the vicinity of July. At some point following this, the rotational system put Caiaphas back into the highest office, which was then ultimately stripped from him by Vitellius.

So, when Luke says that John the Baptist came in the high priesthood of Annas and Caiaphas, he is not saying, suggesting, or even hinting that there were two high priests simultaneously—a legitimate, titled high priest and another high priest operating behind the scenes by public consent. Luke is giving us a dating landmark. It would be similar to a Roman dating a year by the two consuls in office. Luke is giving his reader a very specific year, up to and including the sequence in which the two men served.

When you consider all the nuances discussed regarding bribes, patronage, years-long retention of incumbency, etc., this reference might be even more specific than we realize. If incumbents typically retained the office for many years at a time, with only occasional interruptions, then the specific year when Annas, and then Caiaphas, held the office could very well be unique within the context of the other temporal markers.

Point of fact, since Annas would have been serving the administrative year 27–28 CE, it is highly probable that Pilate installed him in place of Caiaphas in the summer of 27 CE upon his arrival. Like so many governors before him, he would have wanted to assert his authority, resulting in this sequence between Annas and Caiaphas.

In consideration of the full scope of the evidence, the mechanism behind Luke's statement is a case of complicated simplicity. Despite the hoops people have jumped through to make sense of this dual high priest scenario, the solution, in the end, amounts to nothing more than a simple calendrical overlap. What appears to the modern scholar to be a statement contrary to known Jewish practice turns out, in fact, to be a more historically astute chronological reference than Luke has been given due credit for. What generations of scholars have viewed with curiosity, skepticism, or even disdain turns out to be precisely the sort of locally informed detail we have come to expect from Luke.

This fresh look at his intimate knowledge of local Jewish culture and the political environment also sheds additional light on related arguments, such as Luke's ethnicity and the meaning of the "fifteenth year of the reign of Tiberius Caesar." Luke's overtly Jewish references make it clear that he was either himself Jewish, or was a tradent recorder faithfully documenting information being given to him by a Jew. The overall grouping leaves no doubt about the source of the information. We have Zacharias and the course of Abijah. We have Pontius Pilate, the local Judaean Praefect. We have Antipas, Philip, and Lysanias, all local tetrarchs. And we have two high priests listed in a sequence that could very well indicate a specific and potentially unique year, depending on the temporal specifics. All of these references are definitively Jewish. They would have been recognized by any Jew contemporary to the time in question, whereas the average Gentile would have been ignorant of the majority of them.

However, let the proposed solution to the high priests of Luke 3:2 suffice. The other topics are matters for future study.

Bibliography

Balsdon, J. P. V. D. *Life and leisure in Ancient Rome*. London: Phoenix Press, 2002.

Beard, Mary, John North, and Simon Price. *Religions of Rome*. Vol. 1, *A History*. Cambridge: Cambridge University Press, 1998.

Bowman, Alan K. *The Town Councils of Roman Egypt*. American Studies in Papyrology 11. Toronto: A. M. Hakkert Ltd., 1971.

Brown, Raymond E. *The Gospel According to John (XIII–XXI)*. Anchor Bible 29A. Garden City, NY: Doubleday, 1970.

Bruce, F. F. *The Acts of the Apostles: The Greek Text With Introduction and Commentary*. 3rd rev. and enl. ed. Grand Rapids, MI: Eerdmans, 1990.

Catchpole, David R. *The Trial of Jesus: A Study in the Gospels and Jewish Historiography from 1770 to the Present Day*. Leiden: E. J. Brill, 1971.

Clarke, Adam. *The New Testament of Our Lord and Saviour Jesus Christ, with a Commentary and Critical Notes*. Vol. 1. New York: Daniel Hitt and Abraham Paul, 1818.

Drogula, Fred K. *Commanders & Command in the Roman Republic and Early Empire*. Chapel Hill: University of North Carolina Press, 2015.

Edersheim, Alfred. *The Life and Times of Jesus the Messiah*. New updated ed. Peabody, MA: Hendrickson Publishers, 1993.

Eisler, Robert. *The Messiah Jesus and John the Baptist According to Flavius Josephus' Recently Rediscovered "Capture of Jerusalem" and the Other Jewish and Christian Sources*. Translated by Alexander Haggerty Krappe. New York: Dial Press, 1931.

Ellicott, Charles John, ed. *A New Testament Commentary for English Readers*. Vol. 1. New York: E. P. Dutton & Co., 1878.

Enelow, H. G. "Annas." In *The Jewish Encyclopedia: A Descriptive Record of the History, Religion, Literature, and Customs of the Jewish People from the Earliest Times to the Present Day*, edited by Isidore Singer, vol. 1, 610–611. New York: Funk and Wagnalls, 1907.

Fitzmyer, Joseph A. *The Gospel According to Luke I–IX: Introduction, Translation, and Notes*. Anchor Bible 28. New York: Doubleday, 1981.

Fowler, W. Warde. *The Religious Experience of the Roman People from the Earliest Times to the Age of Augustus*. The Gifford Lectures for 1909–10 delivered in Edinburgh University. London: Macmillan, 1911.

Gill, John. *An Exposition of the New Testament, in Three Volumes*. Vol. 1. London: Aaron Ward, 1746.

Henry, Matthew. *Matthew Henry's Commentary on the Whole Bible*. Vol. 5, Matthew to John. McLean, VA: MacDonald Publishing Company, 1970.

Horsley, Richard A. "High Priests and the Politics of Roman Palestine: A Contextual Analysis of the Evidence in Josephus." *Journal for the Study of Judaism in the Persian, Hellenistic, and Roman Period* 17, no. 1 (June 1986): 23–55.

Jamieson, Robert, A. R. Fausset, and David Brown. *A Commentary, Critical and Explanatory, on the Old and New Testaments.* Vol. 2, New Testament. Hartford: S. S. Scranton Company, 1873.

Keener, Craig S. *The IVP Bible Background Commentary: New Testament.* 2nd ed. Downers Grove, IL: InterVarsity Press, 2014.

Mason, Steve. *Josephus and the New Testament.* Peabody, MA: Hendrickson Publishers, 1992.

McEachern, Vernon E. "Dual Witness and Sabbath Motif in Luke." *Canadian Journal of Theology* 12, no. 4 (1966): 267–280.

Plummer, Alfred. *A Critical and Exegetical Commentary on the Gospel According to S. Luke.* Edinburgh: T. & T. Clark, 1896.

Schwartz, Daniel R. *Studies in the Jewish Background of Christianity.* Wissenschaftliche Untersuchungen zum Neuen Testament 60. Tübingen: Mohr Siebeck, 1992.

Scullard, H. H. *Festivals and Ceremonies of the Roman Republic.* Ithaca, NY: Cornell University Press, 1981.

Segal, J. B. "Intercalation and the Hebrew Calendar." *Vetus Testamentum* 7, no. 3 (July 1957): 250–307.

Stern, M. "Aspects of Jewish Society: The Priesthood and Other Classes." In *The Jewish People in the First Century: Historical Geography, Political History, Social, Cultural and Religious Life and Institutions*, vol. 2, edited by S. Safrai and M. Stern, 561–630. Philadelphia: Fortress Press, 1976.

Wolter, Michael. *The Gospel According to Luke.* Vol. 1, *Luke 1–9:50.* Translated by Wayne Coppins and Christoph Heilig. Baylor-Mohr Siebeck Studies in Early Christianity. Waco, TX: Baylor University Press, 2016.

www.ingramcontent.com/pod-product-compliance
Lightning Source LLC
Chambersburg PA
CBHW051243120626
46547CB00014B/1771